GW00601117

TERRITORY OF
HONG KONG

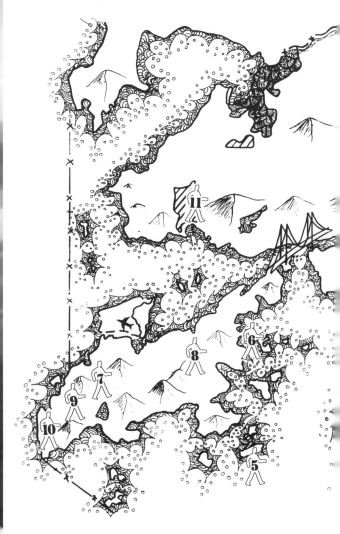

HONG KONG PATHFINDER

Hong Kong
PATHFINDER

Hong Kong
PATHFINDER

written and photographed

by

Martin Williams

Fourth edition

Asia 2000 Limited
Hong Kong

ISBN 962-7160-72-5

Published by Asia 2000 Ltd
302 Seabird House,
22–28 Wyndham Street, Central,
Hong Kong

http://www.asia2000.com.hk/

Typeset with Ventura Publisher in Palatino by Asia 2000
Printed in Hong Kong by Regal Printing

First edition 1995
Second edition 1996
Third edition 1997
Fourth edition 1998

Contents

Escaping the city

Hong Kong is renowned for its tightly-packed high-rises; a thriving business centre, its city life surges along at a frenetic, stressful pace. Yet Hong Kong has a greener, more tranquil side; around 40 percent of the land area is designated as country park — more, people say, than any other territory.

Reaching the greener side is easy. Even the seemingly remote parts are seldom more than a couple of hours from the claustrophobic confines of the city. By combining journeys by car or public transport with walking, you can experience wild, rugged hills, forested valleys, reservoirs and waterfalls, temples and ageing villages, long-abandoned forts and near-uninhabited islands.

All feature in this book, which is based on articles I wrote (and photographed) for the *South China Morning Post* — most appeared in a column called 'A day away'. The walks were done from April to September, a fact reflected in the accounts (that spring and early summer were exceptionally rainy; I refer to bathing in cool streams, which I would not dream of doing in winter). In preparing each edition of this book I have amended and updated the articles.

You do not need any fancy gear to follow the itineraries described here; besides wearing suitable clothing and footwear, the main item to take, especially in summer, is something to drink.

In each chapter I describe an itinerary suitable for a day's outing (perhaps with an overnight stay, as on Ping Chau). Of course, you might cover part of a route, walk an extra length of trail, or combine sections from different chapters, such as by hiking from Lead Mine Pass above Shing Mun to Tai Po Kau, or spend a long weekend doing routes on Lantau.

Particularly if you want to plan alternative routes, you may want to take a map with you. Maps in the Countryside Series produced by the Survey and Mapping Office are useful, and are available from the Government Publications Centre and some bookshops. (The Bibliography lists other books and maps and where to find them.)

Dress to suit the weather, and the conditions expected along the route. Even in summer, I usually wear a long-sleeved shirt and long trousers, together with a sun hat; these guard against the sun, and offer some protection from thorns and mosquitoes. A spare shirt is useful, to change into before returning to the city. Trainers (sneakers) are adequate for walking, though walking boots give better ankle support and should last longer. If you buy boots, it may be worth choosing a pair which have soles with some 'give'; I have found that very hard plastic soles can skid on damp rocks. If rain seems possible, perhaps take a folding umbrella.

Also useful are suncream, perhaps a swimming costume, and mosquito repellent. Mosquitoes favour damp, shady places; few will bother you as you walk, but they can be a nuisance if you halt in woodland.

Depending on the route, you may wish to carry a picnic lunch. And, something to drink. Drinking — water or soft drinks — is essential during summer, when dehydration is a risk. If you walk in summer, you may be surprised how much you need to drink, so, unless your route is very short or well served by shops, take plenty; it is no fun becoming increasingly thirsty, with no water left and the next shop some distance away. In summer, you might drink from some upland streams — providing you are sure there is no pollution from upstream settlements or agriculture (I have drunk stream water on occasion, without ill effects).

Autumn is the best season for walking; days are often sunny, with pleasant temperatures and low or moderate humidity. Though the season is underway by September, temperatures may remain high into October, and the most comfortable days are typically in November and early December. Unfortunately, the air at this time tends to be sullied by pollution from across the border and Hong Kong traffic, marring views. Even so, you'll be in cleaner air than in the city; and there are clear spells chiefly, perhaps, just after blustery winds have blown in from the north.

By late December, the cold fronts that in autumn invariably bring clear, dry days may instead be followed by grey skies; with no sun, the days may be chilly, sometimes with drizzle.

This grim weather is typical of January and February: as the northeast monsoon blows, temperatures may barely rise above 10°C. But, even though in some years this weather seems never-ending, there may be welcome sunny spells.

By March, spring is beginning. Though days are warmer, nights may remain chilly, and fogs are common.

April sees the last cool weather for months; there may also be an end to grey weather — though, when it does rain, showers are typically heavier than in winter. Especially later in the month, days may be hot, with temperatures around 30°C.

May and June are warm and humid, often with rainy spells — especially when the southwest monsoon of summer is blowing, or there are tropical storms or typhoons. While these storms may bring deluges, and strong winds (hurricane-force if there is a direct hit by a typhoon), the weather while they build over the South China Sea is fine and hot. Because of the higher rainfall, these months can be good for visiting waterfalls. But, if you go walking, take it easy: the heat and humidity are energy-sapping.

Temperatures peak around the second half of July and first half of August. Walking is tough at this time.

But the air can be wonderfully clear; combined with lush summer greenery, this can make for stunning views. Should you head out, maybe choose shorter routes and/or aim for higher places (such as around Ngong Ping on Lantau, where temperatures can be pleasant if there's a good breeze), be prepared to sweat plenty, and be wary of heatstroke.

Towards the end of August, early mornings are a little cooler ('cooler' may mean 26–28°C at sunrise), as autumn begins.

Not surprisingly, there are few people walking the longer trails during summer. At other times of year, trails may be quiet on weekdays, but fairly busy at weekends and during public holidays.

If you travel by public transport, you will find there is a great variety to choose from. The MTR (Mass Transit Railway), serving northern Hong Kong Island, Kowloon and north Lantau, has stations from which you can take other transport to the countryside; so too the KCR (Kowloon-Canton Railway), which runs between Kowloon (Hung Hom station) and the border with Shenzhen. There is an interchange between the MTR and the KCR at Kowloon Tong; to avoid crowded carriages on the KCR, travel first-class.

There are also ferries (as we go to press in 1998, Hong Kong Ferry Company operates most major routes, but franchises are due for tender in spring 1999; the Hong Kong Tourist Association should have up-to-date information), buses and minibuses (on all buses, and green-striped minibuses, no change is given), and taxis. If your attempt at pronouncing a place name is not understood, show a driver the Chinese characters (as on the maps in this book) for your destination.

The Hong Kong Tourist Association is a useful source of information on transport and various sites of interest, telephone 2807-6177.

Hong Kong is a fast-changing place; several of the localities I have described may soon look very different — notably Sha Lo Tung, site of a planned residential development, and the north coast of Lantau, which is being devastated by work associated with the new airport. I welcome readers' comments, regarding any changes to landscape or routes, or suggestions for other walks. (Write to Martin Williams, c/o Asia 2000 Ltd, 302 Seabird House, 22–28 Wyndham Street, Central, Hong Kong.)

I wish to thank friends including Richard Lewthwaite, Malcolm Goude and Numi Goodyear, who introduced me to many fine places in Hong Kong, Charles Anderson and Mike Currie of the *South China Morning Post*, who encouraged me while I was working on the columns, Yka Aaltola for making the signpost featured on the front cover, John Eichelberger for sketching the walking figure on the signpost, Wendy Teasdill for drawing the maps and Fabian Pedrazzini, Gloria Baretto and Andrew McAulay for checking sections of text.

Victoria Peak to Aberdee[n]

0 250 500 750 1000
metres

POKFULAM
薄扶林

Pokfulam Reservoir
薄扶林水塘

High West
西高山

Peak Gardens
山頂公園

香港島

Hong Kong Trail

Lugard Road
盧吉道

Victoria Peak
太平山

夏力道 Harlech Road

同樂徑 Governor's Walk

Mt Austin Rd
柯士甸山道

山頂纜車 Peak Tramway

港島徑

奇力山 Mount Kellett

Hong Kong Trail

遊客節前中心 Park Visitor Centre

ABERDEEN
香港仔

香港仔上水塘
Aberdeen Lower Reservoir
香港仔下水塘

Aberdeen Upper Reservoir

CENTRAL
中環

N

Victoria Peak to Aberdeen

The wild west   *11.5km*

At its start, by the upper Peak Tram station, Mount Austin Road looks as if it might be just another road to a residential district. But alongside it are trees and open spaces, as well as apartment blocks, and soon after starting up the road, I reach a bend with a view bettering that from the tram station.

It is a familiar view — across Central, Wanchai, Victoria Harbour and Kowloon — but, if months have passed since I last visited, I can always play spot-the-new-building, or new expanse of reclaimed land.

I leave the apartment blocks behind and, on reaching Victoria Peak Gardens, turn to the left, along the Governor's Walk. The path crosses a stream, and leads away from the manicured gardens, to curve round the hillside, to the other, wilder side of Hong Kong Island.

The city now seems remote. There are no buildings by the path; just trees and shrubs. Woodland ripples across the hillside: many of the trees were planted to regulate water flowing to Pokfulam Reservoir in the valley below.

I reach a junction, and take a detour to the top of Victoria Peak Gardens and a viewpoint with an impressive vantage across the harbour, and west towards Lantau, Cheung Chau and other islands.

Then, back down the steps, and on to where Lugard and Harlech Roads meet. I join the Hong Kong Trail, which has wound round Lugard Road from its start at the Peak Tram station. It leads westwards, along the north slopes of High West. After a rest area, the trail turns down, and south.

The city is close again; I can hear air-conditioners in Pokfulam high-rises that are almost level with the path. I enter woodland, and the high-rises are lost from view.

The path runs up and round to the left. I cross streams cascading down to the reservoir. At the main stream, the path turns sharp right, almost doubling back on itself as it hugs the valley contours.

There is another uphill section. Then a valley overgrown with tall, dense grass. Maybe it was cultivated until quite recently, and trees are yet to assert themselves. With a low ridge hiding Pokfulam, it seems a secret place.

Along this stretch of the trail, there is little shade. I soak my shirt with water from a stream: air-conditioning for summer hikers.

Woodland again. A squirrel shrieks in alarm, scampers higher in a tree, then sits and watches as I pass.

The path runs downhill, follows a formerly 'difficult' section made easier by steps, and takes me round a sharp spur, to a hillside overlooking Aberdeen. It is a noisy place, with a continuous racket from traffic and construction work. The nearest buildings are only a couple of hundred metres away.

The path runs alongside a catchwater bound for Aberdeen Upper Reservoir. After curving to the right, it crosses the catchwater. A sign shows the Hong Kong Trail leading up a valley. Instead, I turn right almost immediately, where arrows painted in red point up a flight of steps: a short cut.

At a junction, more red arrows point upwards. The slope then eases. I reach the Hong Kong Trail again, and turn right.

Much as when I was near Pokfulam Reservoir, I find myself on a woodland trail, roughly following the contours of the hillside. Many of the trees here were also planted, to improve the Aberdeen reservoirs' watershed. But there is nothing regimented about these woods; the thriving wild plants include creepers growing in dense tangles beneath the canopy. If not for the sounds of Aberdeen, which fade as I walk along, this path could be far from city life.

I leave the Hong Kong Trail where a signpost indicates a track to the right leads to Aberdeen Reservoirs, 300 metres away. Soon, I arrive by the upper reservoir, which at last has a respectable water level. I take a road towards Aberdeen. At first, it keeps to the catchwater I followed before the short cut; the catchwater is wider here, swollen by waters from further tributaries. After turning left, and gently down, the road passes the Aberdeen Country Park visitor centre.

I stop to rest, and look at the centre's exhibits. They seem dated, with some questionable information on wildlife. Still, the air conditioning is pleasant.

Then, to the edge of Aberdeen, and a taxi back to Central.

Getting there

The Peak Tram is probably the most convenient way of reaching the upper tram station.

From outside Aberdeen Country Park (on Aberdeen Reservoir Road), take a taxi, buses 7 (to Central) or 76 (Causeway Bay), or minibuses 4A or 4C (Causeway Bay) or 4B (Wanchai).

Take food and drink: other than a kiosk at the top of Victoria Peak Gardens (closed when I visited), there are no shops en route.

The route is well signposted. The Countryside Series map *Hong Kong Island* is useful; from it, you can find many alternative routes.

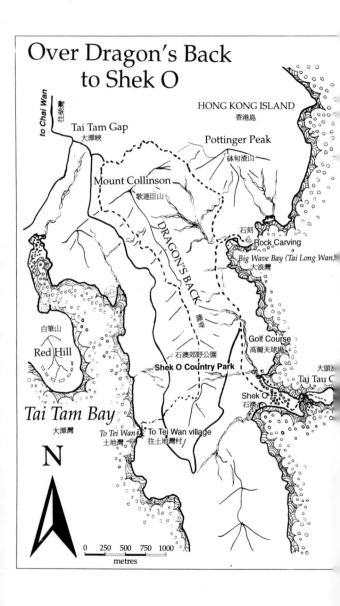

Over Dragon's Back
to Shek O

to Chai Wan 往柴灣

HONG KONG ISLAND
香港島

Tai Tam Gap
大潭峽

Pottinger Peak
砵甸渣山

Mount Collinson
歌連臣山

DRAGON'S BACK
龍脊

石刻
Rock Carving

Big Wave Bay (Tai Long Wan)
大浪灣

白筆山
Red Hill

石澳郊野公園
Shek O Country Park

Golf Course
高爾夫球場

大頭洲
Tai Tau C

Shek O
石澳

Tai Tam Bay

大潭灣

To Tei Wan 土地灣　**To Tei Wan village** 往土地灣村

N

0　250　500　750　1000
metres

Over Dragon's Back to Shek O

Squiggles on a rock face   *10km*

As the taxi winds its way up the ridge above Chai Wan, the city slips away. Soon, there is woodland on both sides of the road. The taxi turns left, and passes a sign announcing SHEK O COUNTRY PARK. Ahead, I see the number 9 bus, bound for Shek O. As I am, eventually.

We pass a small car park on the right, wind along the hillside, turn left past a tiny park on the right, and stop above the hamlet of To Tei Wan. On the right, a sign indicates a path TO DIETY BEACH. On the left is a notice board with a map: section eight of the Hong Kong Trail starts here, and should take around 2¾ hours.

Stone steps lead uphill, to the ridge called Dragon's Back. I pass the ruins of a small house, where a dog barks and scuttles off. A signpost points the way up the hillside, which today belongs only to birds, and me. Soon, I am on the exposed spine of the dragon.

Wind-pruned grasses and shrubs carpet the ridge. Below the steep eastern slope is Shek O: close enough that I can hear the sounds of traffic, yet somehow remote from this hilltop trail. The gentler west slope runs down to Tai Tam Bay; across the water is Stanley, and a grim, faceless cluster of new houses on Red Hill. Beyond them lie wooded hills and reservoirs.

After snaking north along the ridge, the Hong Kong Trail turns left, and down. The sheltered west slopes of Dragon's Back are clothed in young forest. Spring has arrived: some of the trees are tinged red with new leaves, others are brighter — greener — than their neighbours.

The trail levels off, and winds through the trees. I reach a junction, where a narrow road meets my track, now itself concrete. The road passing through Tai Tam Gap is close by, offering an easier way to reach the trail here for anyone feeling unfit, or lazy. A sign beside the track I have just walked down warns of difficult hiking on the Dragon's Back; I found it straightforward, and think the trail planners were being too cautious.

Now, the Hong Kong Trail follows the access road, before turning off down steps to Big Wave Bay (Tai Long Wan). I find little of interest in either the walk or the views, and am glad to reach the bay.

I pass houses where Sunday mahjong sessions are well underway, and look across fields and low buildings to the grey hillside I've just left. Bring someone here who did not know the place, and they might guess they were in the darkest New Territories.

There is serious barbecuing going on in a small park. A shack offers food and drinks, and the menu of a shop facing the beach lists eight noodle dishes.

The sand is pale, the water blue — looking surprisingly clear and inviting to anyone used to the fetid brown broth that slops round most of the territory's coastline. But with a red flag up, and the sea still cool, no one is swimming. There are showers here; even if you don't swim, you may find them useful after the hills.

My map indicates a rock carving on the bay's north headland. A concrete path has been built to it, and I go to look. Ancient it might be, but I reckon only an archaeologist could be inspired by the carving which, housed in its own shelter, is just squiggles on a rock face.

Leaving Big Wave Bay, where the sea is disappointingly calm, I walk along the road towards Shek O. Big driveways lead off to big fancy houses, or to mansions hidden among trees.

The road cuts between golf course fairways. I see two little old ladies, in Hakka garb and galoshes, carrying bags with woods, irons and putters. Golf for the proletariat, just as they had forecast! But look again; they are caddying for taipans and tai-tais.

Kamikaze cyclists of kindergarten age weave among the traffic, making death-defying U-turns that suggest none holds that prized award of my youth — a Cycling Proficiency Badge.

And so to Shek O, and a first impression of round-about, traffic, tourists, and restaurants. The main road of the village, town, or whatever this place is, runs westwards. Traffic moves fitfully, squeezing between buildings, parked cars and strolling pedestrians. At the tip of the headland, the hotchpotch of houses gives out.

There is a footbridge across to a small, rugged island — Tai Tau Chau. Floating refuse has found a resting place in the channel between island and headland; polystyrene litters the shore.

The concrete path builders have been here, too, easing the way to barbecue sites and the lookout pavilion on the island's summit. The top of the southern cliffs is a good place to sit, rest, and look at the view.

A good place for intimate moments, too. I pass a couple who have found an alternative to barbecuing, and walk back to the headland. Just south of the headland, people play frisbee, football and volleyball on the beach. In north Shek O are ramshackle houses along narrow streets, a small, ageing temple, a woman washing vegetables under a standpipe.

I clamber into a minibus, which leaves once full, and takes me back to Shau Kei Wan MTR station, and the big city.

Getting there

To reach the start of the route, take a minibus, taxi, or bus 9 bound for Shek O, from near Shau Kei Wan MTR station, and get out above To Tei Wan. To join the route after the Dragon's Back section, get out near Tai Tam Gap, by the sign indicating SHEK O COUNTRY PARK. Minibuses and bus 9 depart Shek O for Shau Kei Wan.

Carry plenty of water or soft drinks: there are no stalls until Big Wave Bay. Especially if you walk on Dragon's Back, wear footwear with a good grip (trainers should be fine).

The trail is well marked. If you want to take a map, the best is the Countryside Series map *Hong Kong Island*. The leaflet on the Hong Kong Trail is also useful.

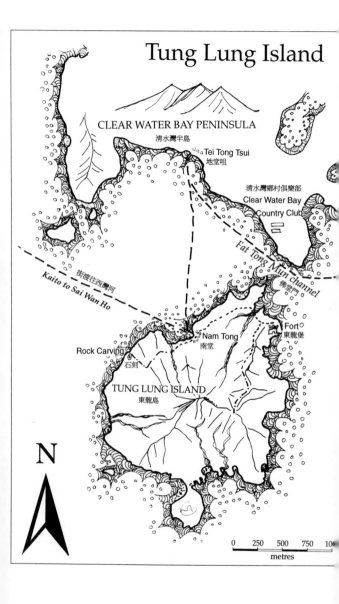

Tung Lung Island

Where rock climbers dare   *3km*

Tung Lung Fort was surely a grim place to be posted. The lifestyle was austere, with cramped living quarters, few other people on the island, and supplies perhaps infrequent. The fort's location, on a low, east-facing headland, exposed it to most monsoons, storms and typhoons that blew in. And to attacks by bands of pirates and rogue troops.

But, largely because of its setting, the fort is a fine place to visit. From information I have read, I know it to be partly renovated ruins. Sure enough, I find that little remains except a squat wall enclosing a rectangular space. From an entrance, a modern wooden walkway leads part way in, and overlooks the interior. Of the walls which once separated the 15 rooms, only the bases remain; they have been exposed by archaeologists, and pattern the floor. Overhead, there is a protective covering of corrugated sheeting, complete with skylights and drainage pipes.

Outside, there are steps to a viewing platform on the thickest part of the wall. Cannons were perhaps sited here, to help guard the narrow channel between Tung Lung and the Clear Water Bay peninsula.

Across the channel is the Clear Water Bay Golf and Country Club, with its imposing main building and manicured golf course. Then hills, with High Junk Peak dominating the peninsula. To the right, Steep Island appears well named. Further east, the fort's headland looks out across the sea and occasional islands.

I guess the sea view was one of the reasons the fort was sited on this headland, rather than on the island's northernmost promontory. Besides guarding the Fat

Tong Mun channel, which was used by Canton-bound trading junks, the garrison was ideally placed for watching the waters east of Hong Kong, and signalling the approach of attacking forces.

When the fort was built, on the order of Yang Ling, Viceroy of Guangdong and Guangxi from 1719 to 1724, these forces could have included troops still loyal to the deposed Ming Dynasty. There were pirates, too: three pirate bands are rumoured to have attacked the fort, before, isolated and superseded, it was evacuated in 1810.

I start on a path towards the island's main peak. On my left are inlets and cliffs; on the right, a treeless hillside, and a crumbling house low in a valley. The path becomes overgrown; I tell myself dangerous snakes are mostly active at night, and push on.

I stop abruptly. Just in front of me, at around knee height, there is a thin green line among the leaves and branches. A bamboo snake. It is motionless, and apparently unaware of me. Two more paces, I think, and I would have walked into it: I could have been bitten. Though only half a metre long, the snake could have injected a painful venom (the bite is not fatal to most adults).

When I brush against leaves, the snake drops out of sight. Quickly, I step back. Abandoning plans for visiting the peak — and seeing the island's highest cliffs — I walk down.

Turning from the main path, I follow trails above lower, but still dramatic, cliffs. I step onto a boulder, and peer over the edge. A wall of rock drops sheer away from me, to the waters of a narrow inlet. Opposite is another cliff, the edge of a narrow spur defying the sea. Beyond, and lower than the spur, is the fort headland.

I walk round the head of the inlet, and onto the spur. From here, I can watch rock climbers. Novices are clambering up the low cliffs below the fort. Two, perhaps more experienced, climbers have walked onto the head of the inlet, and are starting up the highest section of the rock wall. One of them sits and waits while the other leads, suspending himself from a sling hanging from pitons he hammers into the rock.

Near the fort, I rest in a shelter overlooking the sea. I hear mynahs calling, waves lapping on rocks. New Age people might pay serious money for such tranquility.

I walk back to the hamlet of Nam Tong, where I landed on the island, and buy a drink at a ramshackle restaurant. A little way south, there is a rock carving above the shore. From the boat coming in, I saw a concrete path leading down to the carving, which is apparently screened from the elements.

A sign points the way, and I set off. First, I am on an old concrete path. But, beside farmhouses which seem abandoned — I have seen just six island residents today, all of them elderly — the path deteriorates, and tunnels through low trees. I walk on, but decide there is too much undergrowth to push through, and return to the hamlet, to await the kaito back to Sai Wan Ho.

I am not too concerned about missing the carving. Maybe, as people have suggested, it represents a dragon. But from photos I see, it is just swirling lines; a product, perhaps, of too much time spent chasing the dragon, or in enforced island isolation.

Getting there

Tung Lung Island is reached by ferry or kaito from Sai Wan Ho.

The ferry only operates at weekends and on public holidays, departing Sai Wan Ho at 8:30 AM and 3:30 PM on Saturdays and 8:30 AM and 9:45 AM on Sundays and public holidays, and Tung Lung Island at 4 PM on Saturdays, and 1 PM, 2 PM, 3 PM and 4 PM on Sundays. Return fare is $20.

To reach the ferry: take Exit A (Tai On Street) from Sai Wan Ho MTR station, turn right, keep straight on to near the bus terminus, then turn right again following the quayside for about 100 metres, looking out for the ferry which, as we go to press, is a little blue and white contraption with scaffolding serving as the upper deck railing. For information on ferries, telephone 2560-9929 (Cantonese only).

Hire kaitos by asking at the waterfront for 'Tung Lung Chau'. Agree a price (I paid $300) and pick-up time; pay after the return trip.

Drinks and noodles are available in the hamlet; the Hop Huen Store rents bungalows with air conditioning (telephone 2564-3646, Cantonese only, accommodation likely to be basic).

The track to the fort is signposted. An information hut by the fort is open daily except Tuesdays.

Tung Lung is included in the Countryside Series map *Outlying Islands,* and there is a brochure available from the Antiquities and Monuments Office.

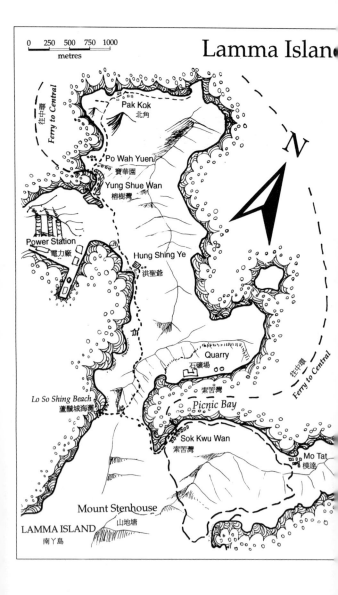

Lamma Island

Pier to pier   *5km*

As the ferry nears Sok Kwu Wan, the east coast of Lamma appears near unspoiled — hills run down to a coast with clusters of houses. But when we enter Picnic Bay for the final approach, the island presents a different face: a huge quarry scars the inlet's north side; below the retreating cliff are cement works.

The ferry berths on the inlet's unscathed southern shore. The village of Sok Kwu Wan, just six kilometres from Aberdeen, is dominated by a row of seafood restaurants that cater to junk parties.

Signposts for the Lamma Family Trail point left and right from the ferry pier. To the left lies Mo Tat village, on a loop which takes in old fields, a quiet coastline, and the east flank of Mount Stenhouse, Lamma's highest peak.

I turn right, on a route which will take me to the other ferry pier, at Yung Shue Wan. I pass restaurants where staff are making ready for lunchtime trade, then a small temple, and trees with roots sprawling across boulders.

The path crosses a stream and turns north. Beside it, there are tunnels cut into the foot of the hillside, reputedly during the Japanese occupation — a trail sign calls one CAVE KAMIKAZE.

At a school, and just before the art deco shelter of the Lo So Shing sitting out area, I turn left, through a break in the hills. The low, flat land is patterned with banana groves, fields and marshes; above the school, and the houses on the opposite slopes, are woods and grassy hilltops.

Reaching a junction, I take the path to Lo So Shing Beach, on the west coast of Lamma. Set in a bay backed by low, wooded hills, the beach affords fine views to Cheung Chau and Lantau Islands. Views tempered by the power station, which looms over the bay's northernmost headland.

From a rocky promontory, southern Lamma is still wild, with rugged Mount Stenhouse dropping steeply to the sea. The beach looks clean here; the water quality was recently given a Grade One rating. All that is needed for swimming is Grade One weather.

My map shows trails leading north from the beach. I make half-hearted attempts at finding them, beyond the block with showers and toilets. Failing, I return to the family trail and turn north again, through the village of Lo So Shing.

The path climbs, leaves the woodland, and I am above one of the grim cement works. Minutes later, the works hidden from view, the path rambles across west-facing slopes dotted with boulders that have made it only part way to the sea.

After a pavilion, the path leads gently down, to the beach at Hung Shing Ye. This faces the power station, which seems immense, and alien — the sort of place Schwarzenegger might battle killer robots.

There are three-storey apartment blocks above the beach: lying 20 minutes away from the northern pier for ferries to Central, Hung Shing Ye is expanding as weekenders and commuters move in.

Walking north, I pass through a landscape which is also changing as north Lamma becomes, increasingly, a Hong Kong suburb and retreat from high price, high pressure housing. Fields are disappearing, village boundaries blurring, as new housing is built to cash in on the trend.

Westerners are prominent among the new arrivals. SALE—COME IN announces one of the hand-written signs at a small shop. Among the goods on offer are flapjacks and lasa; none of the signs is in Chinese.

Yung Shue Wan is a huddle of houses and terraces beside its bay. The footpath that serves as the high street is lined with market stalls, shops, bars and restaurants. Inevitably, the restaurants offer an abundance of seafood; also, on some menus, Sunday roast beef.

The village ends by the ferry pier, where I walk up steps between houses, and rejoin the family trail. A sign points the way to Po Wah Yuen and Pak Kok, Lamma's northernmost point.

As the path levels out, the houses end, and Lamma is quiet again. On the hillside above, black drongos perch on rocks or make acrobatic sallies after insects.

The path crests a ridge, next to a rain shelter beside a picnic site. Round a corner to the east are rolling fields with villages named after Pak Kok. I head for the point but, from close to, it looks uninteresting. So back to the ferry pier.

En route, I take a path which leads beyond the rain shelter to a boulder-strewn hilltop. This is a good place to rest, and enjoy the day's finest views of Lamma, with Mount Stenhouse as backdrop to inlets, headlands and villages (only the tops of the power station's chimneys are in sight).

I return to Yung Shue Wan, with time to spare before the ferry to Central.

Getting there

Hong Kong Ferry operates ferries between Central and Sok Kwu Wan and Yung Shue Wan. Also, there are licensed ferries between Aberdeen and Sok Kwu Wan and Yung Shue Wan, and services link Yung Shue Wan to Pak Kok to Kennedy Town.

The Countryside Series map *Outlying Islands* is useful.

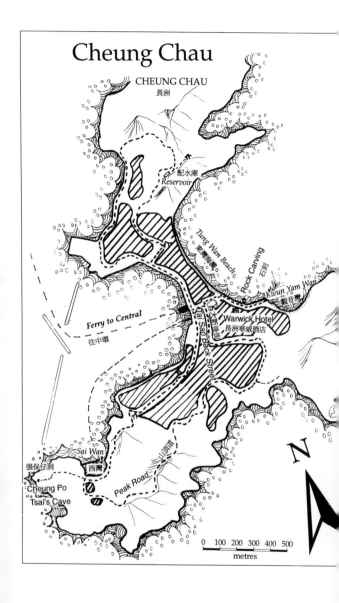

Cheung Chau

Isle of the Northern King   *8.5km*

As you arrive at Cheung Chau, the ferry passes fishing junks moored in the typhoon shelter; the island retains a thriving fishing community. If it is early on a weekday morning, you will have passed ferries packed with people bound for Central; Cheung Chau is also home to increasing numbers of commuters.

The island is formed by two lumps of granite, linked by a low causeway running north-south. The pier, and much of the housing, is on the causeway.

There are no cars on Cheung Chau. Bicycles and pedal carts are available for hire, but — like the Daleks thwarted in their plans to conquer the universe — are of little use when faced with the frequent steps. The best way of getting around is by walking.

If you want to explore, head left or right from the pier; if the beach is your aim, head for the opposite shore of the causeway.

Walking along the waterfront to the left takes you past rows of shops and restaurants, which give way to a football pitch. Turn right here, and you arrive at Pak Tai Temple, where the island's chief god, Pak Tai (the North King), gazes out to the sea.

Each spring, the temple and the basketball court below it become the focus of the Bun Festival. Bamboo, string and tin sheets are fashioned into a grand shed for operas and ceremonies by priests, a shelter for three gods, and the towers which hold the steamed buns.

Part homage to Pak Tai, who is credited with stemming two outbreaks of plague, the festival is also a grand exorcism: after wandering ghosts have feasted on the buns, they are banished to the underworld.

A path leads uphill from beside the temple, passing under an archway noting HOME FOR THE AGED. Not everyone living beyond the archway is aged, though they might feel it after climbing the flight of steps.

The steps lead to a small, concrete-covered playground. From here, turn right, and uphill again. You soon leave the housing behind, and reach grassy hills.

Pass the service reservoir, and there is a track to a hilltop pavilion, with views over Cheung Chau, and to Lamma, Hong Kong Island, and across to Lantau.

A wide track curves down the side of a valley where small farms are set among trees and bamboo, and a new housing development in the lower reaches. It meets a coast road, often busy with cycles and pedal carts.

Turn left at the junction, and you will soon pass an ice factory, and return to 'town'.

Back to the ferry pier. From the public pier beside this you can catch a sampan to the village of Sai Wan, near the southwest tip of the island. Or you could walk, turning right soon after a public pier, to follow the waterfront, then left to a Tin Hau temple, then right passing a new housing estate.

Signposts at Sai Wan show the way over a headland to Cheung Po Tsai's Cave, which you can also reach via a small temple. Cheung Po Tsai was a 19th century pirate, commanding hundreds of vessels and raiding shipping along the south China coast. But, despite local folklore saying he cached his booty here, there is no solid evidence to link him with cave, which is little more than a cleft in the rock.

From above the cave, a narrow flight of steps drops steeply between trees and boulders. This is the beginning of a new path that runs south then east along the coast, to a narrow cove where you have to scramble over rocks (this may be difficult or impassable at high tide), then continues by a rocky headland, and reaches a secluded beach, where a path leads up beside trees and an abandoned farmhouse.

Less interesting, but shorter and easier, is the path that runs through Sai Wan, southwards and away from the harbour at first, then turns eastwards, and meets the path from the beach.

Whichever route you have taken, continue eastwards along Peak Road, which winds gently uphill, then along the crest of southwestern Cheung Chau.

Rural at first, the path soon leads through a construction site, then returns to the main residential area — a sure sign you are nearing the ferry pier. A right turn offers the chance to walk a loop in the Cheung Chau trail, passing more coastal scenery, and boulders with fanciful names (Human Head Rock, Vase Rock and Bell Rock).

Keep straight on, and you reach a downhill stretch. On the right of this part, hidden by rank vegetation at the base of a large tree, is a marker for an old residential boundary, which was aimed at keeping the southern part of Cheung Chau a classy area (much as on Hong Kong Island's Peak, this may have meant excluding Chinese). Nowadays, of course, the whole island is classy, and the ferry journey helps deter riff-raff from taking up residence.

Peak Road ends at a junction soon after the Royal Hong Kong Jockey Club. Should you head to the left, you could wander Cheung Chau's winding, narrow streets. You might also get lost.

Better, then, to turn right into Tai San Back Street, and keep on until you reach the sacred banyan, credited with maintaining the island's prosperity. Some islanders have reportedly adopted it as godfather to their children, hoping they will grow up smart and strong.

Turn right at the tree, and you will come to Tung Wan Beach. Right again and, below Cheung Chau's largest building, the Warwick Hotel, you will find the ancient rock carving.

After gazing in awe at the carving, walk on a little, and take a seat at the Windsurfing Centre, a popular place for a drink on balmy summer afternoons.

In the bay, there may be windsurfers doing their thing. Or trying, anyway — in summer, there is often little wind (zealots await near-misses by typhoons); the best season is autumn, with its gusty cold fronts. If it is summer, the nearby beaches may be crowded; they have showers to wash away any crud that might stick to you if you swim.

The sun drops behind Lantau, and it is time for dinner. Cheung Chau boasts an abundance of seafood restaurants: try along the road with the sacred tree, or along the waterfront. As the evening wears on, waterfront noodle stalls become open air bars. Long past your bedtime, they will be serving beers to thirsty islanders. There may be ribaldry, as imbibers become tired and emotional; but you will never know, for, if you are to return home tonight, you have a ferry to catch.

Getting there

Hong Kong Ferry has ferries between Central and Cheung Chau, and (at weekends and on public holidays) between the island and Tsim Sha Tsui. There is also a ferry linking Cheung Chau with Lantau and Peng Chau a few times a day.

Operators of sampans from near the Cheung Chau ferry pier to Sai Wan may try to fleece tourists; normal fare is $2–$10 per person. The booklet *Cheung Chau Walking Tour* produced by the tourist association is useful, though too cautious in, say, describing an optional route as 'lengthy and rugged'.

The Cheung Chau Bookshop sells maps of the island (turn right from the ferry, and a short way up the street beside the Timberland shop). You may also find the Countryside Series map *Outlying Islands* useful.

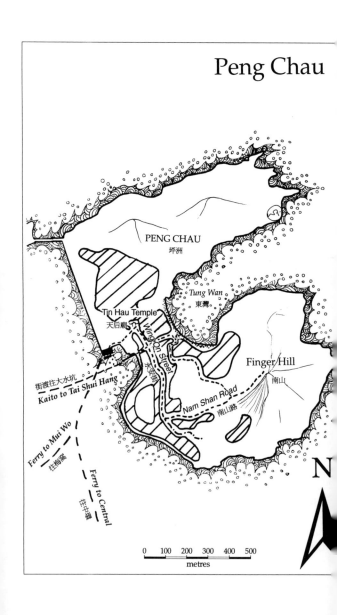

Peng Chau

PENG CHAU
坪洲

Tung Wan
東灣

Tin Hau Temple
天后廟

Wing On Street
永安街

Finger Hill
南山

街渡往大水坑
Kaito to Tai Shui Hang

Nam Shan Road
南山路

Ferry to Mui Wo
往梅窩

Ferry to Central
往中環

N

| 0 | 100 | 200 | 300 | 400 | 500 |
metres

Peng Chau and the Trappists

In search of a quiet life   3km+4km

From Peng Chau's ferry pier, I walk across reclaimed land towards the main village. Reaching a small Tin Hau temple that is hemmed in between buildings, I turn right along Wing On Street.

The street I walk along is narrow, claustrophobic, lined with stores selling fruit, cakes, paper fans, plastic pots, herbal teas and dim sum. Even narrower alleyways lead off to left and right, disappearing into the tight-packed jumble of houses.

There is a gap. Then, the houses are more scattered. The road leads gently uphill.

On the left, NAM SHAM RD is painted on a rock. I take the road, really only a footpath: as on Cheung Chau, there are no cars here.

The path widens to a narrow road lined with villas. With the tiny lawns beside the buildings, it could almost be a cul-de-sac transplanted from Hong Lok Yuen. The first buildings I pass are painted white; then there are some with red archways surrounding rectangular windows; and lastly, there are buildings painted pale mauve, which I suppose someone considered tasteful.

But this isn't a cul-de-sac; the road ends even more abruptly than it started, leading out to a footpath through grass and bushes.

At a junction, I take the path leading straight on, and climb up steps to Peng Chau's highest point, the top of Finger Hill. The steps end at a flat, concrete area, with panoramic views to Hong Kong Island, Lamma, Hei Ling Chau and Lantau.

Nearer, this southern finger of Peng Chau is mostly greenery with occasional farmsteads; across a bay to

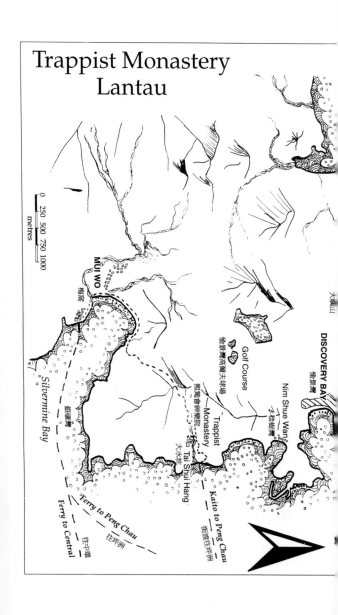

Trappist Monastery
Lantau

0 250 500 750 1000
metres

MUI WO
梅窩

Silvermine Bay
銀礦灣

Ferry to Peng Chau
往坪洲

Ferry to Central
往中環

Golf Course
愉景灣高爾夫球場

Trappist
Monastery
熙篤會神樂院

Tai Shui Hang
大水坑

Kaito to Peng Chau
街渡往坪洲

Nim Shue Wan
稔樹灣

DISCOVERY BAY
愉景灣

大嶼山

the north, the other finger of this horseshoe-shaped island is similarly green, with a large aerial mast near its tip. On the narrow land at the head of the bay is the main village.

I retrace my steps down the hill, and turn right. I reach houses, and turn right again, to a large, youngish temple overlooking the grotty Tung Wan beach.

Then, through narrow streets, a left turn beside the fortress-like Regional Council Complex, and to a small pier. After a short rest, I catch the kaito ferry to the Trappist Monastery on Lantau Island.

I leave the ferry at a solitary pier. Nearby, the stream which flows by the monastery cascades to a beach.

A road curves up and away from the pier. I follow it, through the woodland lining the valley. On some trees are crosses with images of Christ, and numbers that increase as I ascend. By cross number 12 is a building like a school, and a sign reading OUR LADY OF JOY MONASTERY.

I pass another building. On the left, a footbridge leads across the wooded ravine, to the monastery's chapel. TALK IN LOW TONES PLEASE reads a sign before the bridge; on reaching the chapel, SILENCE is requested. For some visitors, a few minutes without speaking might prove difficult; they might reflect on the Trappist monks, sworn to a vow of silence.

I return to the road, pass another bridge, and take a narrow path alongside the stream. On my right are the sheds where the monastery's dairy herd was kept. They are deserted; the cows were moved to Yuen Long, and now the Trappist Dairy brand of milk comes from China.

The path, overgrown in places, crosses the stream and enters more open country. Meeting a wider track, I turn right. I have seen no traffic today, and there are no signs that vehicles have recently used this track, which is disintegrating and sprouting grass. So, among the trees by the track, a wrecked Chrysler car is an unexpected sight.

The track peters out, and I follow a trail uphill. There are views down the valley to the monastery, and across to Peng Chau.

I cut through the gap between two hills. I am high in the rolling, eastern chunk of Lantau; the landscape is spartan, the vegetation dominated by swarthy grass — and the tamer greenery of the Discovery Bay Golf Course on a hill to my right. Below is the sweeping curve of Mui Wo (Silvermine Bay); in the background is Sunset Peak.

From a pavilion on a nearby hilltop, a concrete path drops down to the shore of the bay, which I follow round to the Mui Wo ferry pier.

Getting there

Hong Kong Ferry operates ferries between Central and Peng Chau and Mui Wo (Silvermine Bay); also, at weekends and on public holidays, between Tsim Sha Tsui and Mui Wo.

Kaitos depart Peng Chau for the Trappist Monastery at 11:15 AM, 12:15, 2:20 and 4:15 PM on weekdays; and at 10 AM, 12 noon, 2:30 and 4:30 PM on Sundays and public holidays; services to Nim Shue Wan, only a short walk from the monastery, may be more frequent. There is a timetable at the kaito pier.

The Countryside Series maps *Lantau Island* and *Outlying Islands* (for Peng Chau) are useful.

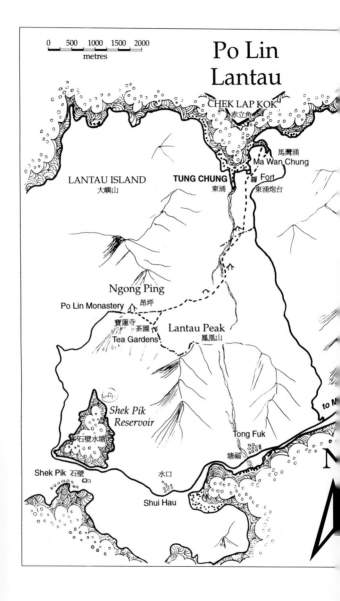

Po Lin

Stairway from heaven   *5km*

For decades, the way to Po Lin Monastery was by the Pilgrim's Path. Beginning at Tai O on the west coast of Lantau, this led halfway up Lantau Peak, to the Ngong Ping plateau. Especially as Lantau was remote and sparsely populated, it was not a route to encourage casual visitors.

Just as well, perhaps. For in the monastery's early years, casual visitors were likely not welcome. Po Lin — or Precious Lotus — was established in 1905 by three reclusive monks who chose the site for their meditations. For shelter, they built stone huts.

How different things are today. Po Lin is now one of the largest, and most visited, monasteries in Hong Kong. It even has its own bus route: the way now begins not at Tai O, but on Lantau's opposite, east shore, at the Mui Wo (Silvermine Bay) ferry pier or on the north shore, at Tung Chung.

I board the bus from Mui Wo on a Saturday and, once the ferry from Hong Kong has arrived, it soon fills with day-trippers and departs. Like a roller coaster being cranked up the initial slope, the bus climbs out of Mui Wo, passing through woodland and by cattle loitering on the verge. Then, we are off, careening along Lantau's southern coast. We pass through Pui O, Cheung Sha, Tong Fuk and Shui Hau. After Shek Pik, the driver tilts at the hill, then turns onto the winding highway that brings Po Lin its visitors, and dollars.

Highway and journey end at an expanse of concrete rivalling the Mui Wo terminus. Beside this, stalls sell drinks, snacks and souvenirs. Nearby is the monastery, modern and colourful. Prominent among the decor —

its image patterns the floor of the main hall — is the lotus flower, important emblem of Buddhist faith. If such beauty can grow from mud and stagnant water, reason Buddhists, anyone can attain enlightenment.

As if to remind visitors of enlightenment — and of the possible short cut to a better after life through making worthy donations — the big bronze Buddha sits on a nearby hilltop, gazing across the bus stop to Po Lin.

A flight of steps leads to the base of the statue (at 26.4 metres 'the largest outdoor bronze statue of Buddha in the world'), from where there are great views of the monastery and surrounding area.

A sign by the bus terminus points to the Tea Gardens. I take the path, which leads through a mix of woodland and tea plantations.

Soon, I reach a paddock, where horse rides are offered. A board lists prices for having a photo taken on horseback, for riding in the paddock, and for riding on trails (minimum three horses).

Then, a cluster of buildings including the Tea Gardens Restaurant — a basic place, where I recall a meal of beer and noodles while mists swirled outside.

A roller skating rink is, as ever on my visits, deserted. I wonder if it was popular at any time.

The trees beside the path give out, and I reach a wooden archway with the legend LANTAU TRAIL. Immediately beyond it rises the sharp cone of Lantau Peak.

I turn left just before the archway, and follow a rough trail. When this meets a concrete path, I turn right, towards Tung Chung.

The path angles down the north slopes of Lantau Peak. Beside a bend in the trail is a pavilion offering a chance to rest, and enjoy the view. There are hills on three sides, while the slopes below me give way to a broad valley with the fields and villages of Tung Chung. Beyond Tung Chung, across a bay, lies the new airport and a small lonesome hill, which is all that remains of Chek Lap Kok, an island sacrificed on the altar of economic progress.

A plane roars overhead. The sound fades, and is lost. A koel and a large hawk cuckoo sing from the wooded hillsides. A gong, struck solemnly and repeatedly, rings out.

The gong is being struck in a pagoda beside a monastery I soon pass. Reached only by footpaths, and set among a stand of larger trees and bamboo, this monastery seems far more suited to a life of contemplation than does Po Lin. Poorer, too: the trail I take leads by another monastery where I see and hear no one, and there are signs of neglect.

There is a wooden sign beside this second monastery, with an arrow pointing down and the letters T.C. — Tung Chung. The path runs steeply down, alongside a stream which has carved a shallow ravine. Then, the slope eases, and the path runs above the ravine before turning right, and down again.

Near the foot of the slope, the path meets a narrow road, and passes the unimposing Lo Hon Monastery. And houses — one of them with soft drinks for sale.

I meet another narrow road, and turn right. This heads for a junction where there are stops for the bus between Mui Wo and Tung Chung. But rather than head for this, I turn left almost immediately, to follow a footpath leading under a stone arch and through the former rice fields. I pass along the front of a three-storey red house, cross a stream, and turn left again.

A later junction, by a shanty farmhouse with vegetable plots, offers a left turn to the little Hau Wong Temple, which looks across to the Chek Lap Kok construction site. Back at the junction, I turn left, eastwards, ignore a path towards seafront shanties, and soon have another choice.

Straight on, the path leads a short distance to the road, and the Tung Chung Fort, where thick walls, one of them topped with cannons, surround buildings housing a school, the rural committee, and a visitor's centre. But I turn left, along the concrete path between damp, old fields — some of which are being readied for construction work — cross a channel, walk between buildings, and am soon on a narrow street lined with shops and restaurants.

A footbridge over the mouth of a creek affords a glimpse of a fishing village that seems a relic of the past, almost quaint — but then, not so long ago, so did the hamlets of Chek Lap Kok. Across the bridge is the bus terminus, and I am soon heading back to Mui Wo.

Getting there

Ferries link Central (and on weekends and public holidays, Tsim Sha Tsui) with Mui Wo (Silvermine Bay). Buses to Po Lin ('Ngong Ping') depart from the Mui Wo ferry pier.

Food and drinks are available at Po Lin and the Tea Gardens; the monastery's vegetarian restaurant is popular.

Buses to Mui Wo depart from the pier at Ma Wan Chung, Tung Chung; there are bus stops along the road leading from the village. Buses to Kowloon leave from Tung Chung new town. They include E31 to Tsuen Wan ferry pier.

From Tung Chung, there are buses to Kowloon and other parts of Hong Kong, and the MTR to stations including Kowloon and Hong Kong Station (in Central).

The Countryside Series map *Lantau Island* is useful.

Tung Chung to Mui Wo

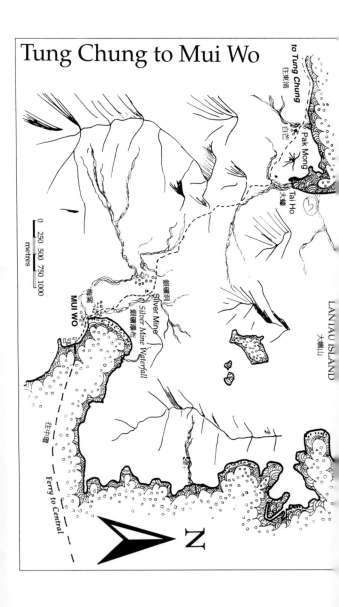

to Tung Chung
往東涌

白芒

Pak Mong

大蠔
Tai Ho

LANTAU ISLAND
大嶼山

梅窩

MUI WO

龍銀坑
Silver Mine
龍銀瀑布
Silver Mine Waterfall

往中環
Ferry to Central

N

0 250 500 750 1000
metres

Tung Chung to Mui Wo

The doomed coast 9.5km

As the airport scheme progressed, the north Lantau coast underwent massive changes. In this account — retained as a gauge of how swift change can be — I relate a walk when the scheme was in its early stages. In 1998, Chek Lap Kok has been reduced to its southernmost rampart and the airport platform with associated buildings, and a new town, a highway, and a giant building site sprawl along the coast east from Tung Chung. The trail passes these, following the inland side of a fence as it runs along the transformaed coastline, reaches Pak Mong — where fierce dogs, perhaps brought in by villagers fearful of construction workers, lurk within the walls — then turns inland, to still-rural Lantau.

From the bus stop by the pier, the fishing hamlet of Ma Wan Chung, Tung Chung still seems a slow, easy place: the kind of place you could visit years later, and still find the same buildings, the same staff in the shops and restaurants, the same people lingering over noodles and dumplings. It's an illusion of course: the 21st century is arriving with a vengeance.

I walk away from the pier, along Tung Chung's road to the outside world. On the left is Tung Chung Battery, which once guarded the approaches to the Pearl River. It is in ruins and undramatic, a broad, angled wall on grassy slopes facing the sea.

The road curves to the right, with views across old paddy fields and scattered villages. Some construction work is underway; men in hard hats are making surveys. One day, if the planners' dreams are realised, there will be a new town here, with housing for 150,000.

I turn left, along a road signposted TAI PO. At first, there are trees by the road. Then, near the coast, machines are landscaping earth banks and roads. Across the water, Chek Lap Kok is being bulldozed and blasted ever flatter.

The road ends. A footpath bears right, along the junction between old fields and the bare earth and tree stumps where land is being cleared. But once I reach the village of Tai Po, I walk along a coastline still untouched by the airport scheme.

I turn right at Tai Po, alongside a stream. Passing a building, I set dogs snarling; they dash about madly, but cannot escape their yard. Then, through a small wood, the path leading uphill, away from the sea, before bending left at a small terrace with banana trees, and running parallel with the unseen coast.

Leaving the shade of the taller trees, the path becomes overgrown, though easy to follow. There are shrubs, more trees, fields belonging to the village.

I reach open, grassy hillside, where the path is clear again. Small, steep streams run down to the sea, where there will be an expressway, and industry built on reclaimed land.

The path becomes concrete; there are handrails as I drop down to low land beside a beach. Heading inland, the path runs by Pak Mong, a secluded village with woodland on three sides. Between path and village is a stout, impressive banyan, its roots clutching a granite boulder for support. Beside it are clusters of incense sticks, some of them in old Coca-Cola tins.

There is a short, gentle uphill stretch, past an abandoned schoolhouse where I hope the spelling does not reflect on former teaching standards. PAK MONG SOHOOL reads a large inscription.

Down to Tai Ho, with its fields and hamlets on land beside an inlet, land slated for a new town with industries and a population of over 100,000. At a junction, I turn right, to follow the path south across Lantau.

The path climbs. The north coast slips away, becoming lost from view as the path eases, runs behind a ridge, and twists its way above the streams which start in this rolling, untamed land. One stream, in a gully right of the path, has a plunge pool below a cascade: a fine place for a cooling dip.

To the right, the view is dominated by the steep, eastern slopes of Sunset Peak. Away to the left are low, remote hills. I reach the top of a slope with a vantage over Mui Wo (Silvermine Bay), where a ferry is turning, leaving for Central.

The path zigzags down the slope, passes fields and farmhouses, then drops down again. Right of the path, there is an entrance to the old silver mine. In use late last century, this is now walled off 10 metres in. A gap in the wall allows bats access to their daytime sanctuary in the dark, cool mine.

From the bottom of the second slope, there is a short path to a pavilion beside Silver Mine Waterfall, the last and finest waterfall along today's route. Soon after, by the main path, a swimming pool on the right looks clear and tempting but, unluckily for me, is private.

A flight of steps leads down to the left, and the path skirts a low, wooded hill with a crumbling watch tower on top. I pass houses and shops, cross the River Silver, and walk along the road to the ferry pier.

Getting there

Tung Chung new town is easily reached by numerous buses or the MTR. From there you can walk or take a taxi to the pier at Ma Wan Chung.

An alternative route to Wa Wan Chung is by ferry from Central, or Tsim Sha Tsui at weekends and on public holidays, to Mui Wo (Silvermine Bay) on Lantau, then bus 3 or a taxi.

Take food and drink: the only place en route where drinks may be on sale is Pak Mong — follow the path leading from the banyan to the end row of houses, and try the first house in this row; be wary of the dogs.

The Countryside Series map *Lantau Island* is useful.

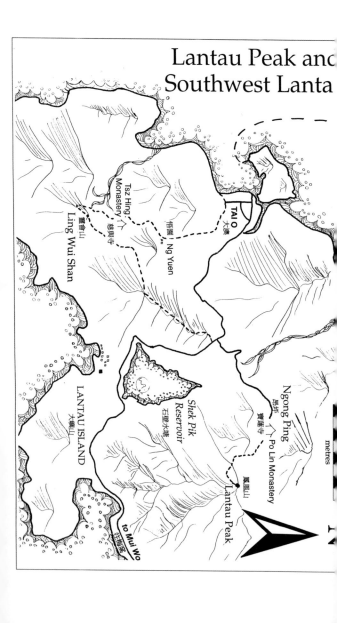

Lantau Peak and
Southwest Lantau

Tsz Hing
Monastery
慈興寺

Ng Yuen
悟園

Ling Wui Shan
靈會山

TAI O
大澳

Ngong Ping
昂坪

Po Lin Monastery
寶蓮寺

LANTAU ISLAND
大嶼山

Shek Pik Reservoir
石壁水塘

Lantau Peak
鳳凰山

metres

to Mui Wo
往梅窩

N

Lantau Peak and Southwest Lantau

Rising sun, flying dragon   *4km+8.5km*

As I leave Ngong Ping's woodland, Lantau Peak looms ahead of me: a black, hulking mass against the night sky. High up the slopes, I can see two points of light, as torches light the way of climbers in the darkness.

There are more lights, more crazy climbers, ahead of me. I follow them, and my torchlight soon picks out the first steps. The first of many steps — I have read that there are 1,400 in all.

Perhaps I have climbed a few hundred of the steps when I halt to rest, and look down at the receding lights of the Tea Gardens, Po Lin Monastery and other buildings at Ngong Ping. I continue: up, up, left and up, as the path turns to follow the spine of an exposed ridge, then a gentler stretch and, at last, I make the final climb to Hong Kong's second highest summit.

Already, a crowd of 50 or more has gathered to wait for the sunrise. A chill wind is blowing: 'Ho tung (very cold)', I hear people saying as they huddle beneath blankets and sleeping bags, and shelter behind rocks.

I find a place away from the worst of the wind, lie back, and look at the night sky — the stars are the brightest I have seen in Hong Kong. A shooting star flashes past, and vanishes, as a tiny meteorite sizzles into nothingness.

With the sun still far away to the east, this high, remote hilltop is a fine place to reflect on life's important questions: Why am I here? Where am I going to? And, why aren't I sound asleep in a nice warm bed?

The crowd stirs as the sky over Hong Kong Island lightens. Cameras are readied in anticipation, but the sun is slow to arrive. Stars flicker out, and the sky turns a pale blue. The sun emerges from behind low clouds, and its yellow tints the South China Sea.

The show over, the audience files down the paths which lead east, and west to Ngong Ping. Back at the Tea Gardens, I return to my room for an hour's sleep. Then, breakfast, and to Po Lin, to catch a bus down the hill.

Twisting down the narrow road, my bus passes others that are bound for Po Lin, and bursting with people. The monastery, which I visited in the calm of yesterday evening, will soon resonate with crowds.

At the junction with the Silvermine Bay to Tai O road, I leave the bus, walk to the left, then start up stage five of the Lantau Trail. There are flights of steps but, when you have climbed 1,400 steps in pitch darkness, they present no challenge.

After reaching a high point, the trail follows a switch-back of grassy hilltops as it aims for Ling Wui Shan — at 490 metres, the highest point in southwest Lantau. Once there, the trail drops down, and turns right.

Soon, on my right, I see the Flying Dragon. A stone and plaster statue, the dragon is a long, spindly beast, balancing on rocks above the Tsz Hing Monastery. Garishly painted, and with its jaws open in a wild roar, it makes a bizarre addition to the landscape.

Past the monastery, which appears otherwise un-remarkable, I reach a stream. The trail crosses it, leads me up the stream valley, then turns away to the right, and reaches another Lantau folly, Ng Yuen.

An ornamental garden in classical Chinese style, Ng Yuen was built by the late Mr Woo Quen-sung. Though privately owned, it is open to the public; I walk in, and stop to buy a welcome, stream-cooled drink. Then, I tour the garden, walking along corridors and grassy paths between summer houses and shrubberies.

While clearly still tended, the garden looks past its best. The houses seem little used, and some of their windows are broken. Perhaps, without Mr Woo's drive and energy, the garden suffers from some neglect — this would be hardly surprising, I think, given the remoteness of the place.

I walk across a zigzag bridge that crosses a lotus pond, and rest at a pavilion above the water. Children throw down bread crusts and crumbs; carp and goldfish swarm in to feed, then cruise through the shallows, waiting for more.

Beside the garden, stage five of the trail ends, and stage six begins. This stage follows a concrete path, which is gentle at first, then drops steeply down to the coast. (For a more pleasant route to the main road — and bus stops — turn right down a concrete path shortly after Ng Yuen, and right again at a catchwater road that hugs contours and affords fine views.)

Reaching a playground, I leave the trail, turning right along a path to Tai O, where I catch a bus to Mui Wo.

Getting there

Hong Kong Ferry operates services between Central and Mui Wo (Silvermine Bay) and, at weekends and on public holidays, between Tsim Sha Tsui and Mui Wo.

Bus 2 departs Mui Wo for Ngong Ping (for many people, the starting point for the trek up Lantau Peak); from Tai O, there are buses to Mui Wo. (Alternatively, take taxis; though these are scarce in Tai O.)

At Ngong Ping, accommodation is available at the Hong Kong YHA's S.G. Davis Ngong Ping Youth Hostel, telephone 2985-5610, with dormitory beds at $45 per night for members and $75 for non-members (a non-member must be accompanied by a member); it closes one or two days a month. There is a four-bed family room at $140.

If you hike up Lantau Peak for the sunrise, take a torch, and be prepared for the cold on the summit.

The Countryside Series map *Lantau Island* is useful.

Fan Lau

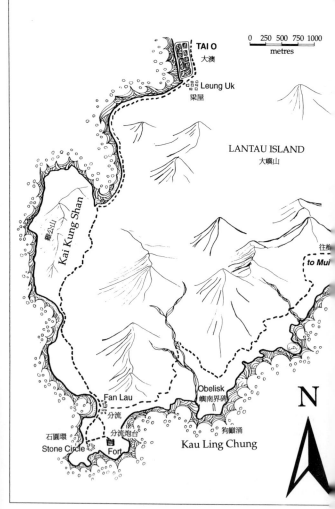

0 250 500 750 1000
metres

TAI O
大澳

Leung Uk
梁屋

LANTAU ISLAND
大嶼山

Kai Kung Shan
雞公山

往梅
to Mui

Fan Lau
分流

Obelisk
嶼南界碑

狗嶺涌

Kau Ling Chung

石圓環
Stone Circle

分流炮台
Fort

N

Fan Lau

Historical relics and soft drinks   *15km*

Fan Lau: the division of flows. A near forgotten outpost of Hong Kong, known mainly for the rumpus over China Light and Power's now abandoned plans for a power station, and an old fort.

I find the fort on a hilltop near the tip of the peninsula. It makes an incongruous sight, spick and span in a corner of Lantau where most buildings are derelict or decaying. There is fresh brick paving, concrete surfacing, and a smart information board.

The board says Fan Lau Fort was built in 1729, and overlooks a strategically important sea passage through the mouth of the Pearl River. It was manned until perhaps 1900, after which it fell into disrepair.

The renovation work, first in 1985, and again in 1990/91, has been thorough. Vegetation which had moved in has been removed; the brick paving will deter further invasion attempts by plant life, as well as protect against wear by visitors' feet. Loose stones have been fixed in place.

I walk through the entranceway and up a flight of steps to the top of a wall. Once, the fort was divided into rooms, but now the walls enclose empty space.

A jetfoil, already half-way to Macau, passes by.

I leave the fort, and head southwest, towards a stone circle. Though also an important historical relic, this has been neglected by the renovators. The path to it is poor; the protective fence has mostly collapsed.

No one knows when or why the circle — which is really an oval — was built. Maybe it is from Neolithic or Bronze Age times, a distant cousin of Europe's great ancient circles. But unlike Stonehenge, say, there is no drama about it — I find the low ring of stones curious but uninspiring.

Below, the water lapping on the east-facing beach looks clearer than the sea beside Fan Lau: this south-west tip of Lantau separates the silty Pearl River from the clearer (but no longer clean) South China Sea.

I return to the village. While at the fort and circle, I had seen no one on the peninsula. I'm not really surprised — even at a brisk walk, the nearest road is a good two hours away.

Longer if you pause en route. I took three hours to reach Fan Lau from Tai O. The route was not tough — for much of it I was on concrete footpaths; where the concrete gave out, there were the slabs and stones of old village trails. Once, there was a short, steep descent above a beach; occasionally, the path ran through damp patches that might be squelchy after heavy rains.

After leaving the hamlets near Tai O, I passed only two or three houses which were obviously still lived in. The trail led through woodland, wound beside small bays, and cut through the gap that nearly separates Lantau from Kai Kung Shan.

Reaching Fan Lau, I took the turning marked FANLAU FORT. Moments later, I was met by a fine sight. SO KEE STORE, a sign announced, BEER AND DRINKS.

In the yard of a small house was a fridge and, with the bottle of water I had brought along already half empty, I reached in for a bottle of orange. 'No, not cold,' the old storekeeper said. The fridge was not working. But another, in the living room, was: it was crammed with cans and bottles, one of which I drained.

After the store came a choice of paths. One, to the beach, seemed a dead end. Another vanished into un-dergrowth. I finally walked past a line of apartments which, though modern, were derelict, and then up a narrow path to the fort.

But the way I find back to the village is better, leading me down to the beach, and so to the store, for another bottled drink.

I have followed the Lantau Trail for most of the way to Fan Lau. Now, one of the trail's yellow markers points me eastwards, away from the cluster of houses.

Soon, I am climbing a trail which angles up and across a steep hillside; below me, Lantau plunges into the sea.

Streams have cut narrow gullies, where signs warn it could be dangerous to cross when they are in flood. But none of the streams is threatening today; some are dry.

A sign points down to a bay with a sandy beach and a campsite. I remain on the Lantau Trail, which curves above the bay, makes a last uphill burst, and levels out to run alongside a catchwater.

Beside the headland east of the bay, stage seven of the Lantau Trail ends, and stage eight begins. There is another path down to the beach; I walk down a little way, and sit on a bench. Boulders rest among vegetation blackened by fire: another path leads to the obelisk on Kau Ling Chung. This was fixed in place in 1902, to mark where the sea boundary with China then touched Lantau. I wonder about going to look, my legs say no, and I stay on the bench.

Then, off again. Though easy going, the catchwater path does not make for pleasant walking: trees obstruct coastal views, while the hillside presents an expanse of scrub, rocks, and plantations.

I plod along, and at last reach the main road by Shek Pik. A bus takes me to Mui Wo, with time to spare for a meal, and very welcome beer.

Getting there

Hong Kong Ferry operates regular ferries between Central and Mui Wo (Silvermine Bay); also weekend and public holiday services between Tsim Sha Tsui and Mui Wo. Buses to Tai O run from the Mui Wo ferry pier; they typically coincide with the arrival of the ferries from Central. Or, you could take a bus or the MTR to Tung Chung, then a bus to Tai O.

From the Tai O bus terminus, follow the path towards villages including Leung Uk; this meets the Lantau Trail.

Buses back to Mui Wo can be caught near the end of the trail at Shek Pik.

Alternatively, try arranging for a boat to take you from Fan Lau back to Tai O. Ng Fook advertises a boat service: telephone 2985-8709 (if you don't know the language, have a Cantonese-speaking friend enquire about, and arrange, the trip: the cost is around $300).

The Countryside Series map *Lantau Island* is useful.

Kowloon from Lion Rock

Climber on Tung Lung Island

Mirror Pool Waterfall

Pak Tai Temple, Cheung Chau

Cheung Chau

Laughing Buddha, Castle Peak Monastery

e at Ham Tin; Sharp Peak behind

Dragon's Back

Tai Po Kau

umn leaves, Shing Mun

Sha Tau, Ping Chau

Ng Yuen, Lantau

Buddha at Po Lin

Lantau Peak

Fan Lau Fort

Tuen Mun

Castle Peak 青山

Castle Peak Monastery 青松觀

TUEN MUN 屯門

Hoh Fuk Tong Centre

N

0 250 500 750 1000
metres

Correctional Services Centre

Castle Peak Road 青山

Tai Lam Chung Reservoir 大欖涌水塘

MacLehose Trail 麥理浩徑

新界

Tuen Mun

Up the peak without a path   *10km*

Though Castle Peak Monastery is only on the outskirts of Tuen Mun, I reach it the easy way, by taxi. This stops at a car park just below the monastery.

Overhead, cables sizzle with electricity from the nearby power station.

I walk up the road past the monastery, then up a footpath. I have arrived with ideas of climbing Castle Peak which, in an imperial decree of 969 AD, was proclaimed a Sacred Mountain. But, close up, the peak looks unappealing, and a fence barring the way easily persuades me to give up on the trek; a sign beside it warns of falling rocks. (I later saw I had missed the way; a winding trail heads towards the communications paraphernalia perched on the summit.)

Easier then to just explore the monastery, which I had planned to visit on the way down. Though the current buildings date from 1918, this is one of the two oldest monasteries in Hong Kong, dating back over 1,500 years.

To my eyes, the buildings hold the typical trappings of Buddhism: statues, pictures, incense sticks; a rack of shelves houses papers with answers for fortune tellers. In one building, there is a small fountain, with the jets of water piped from kitschy, miniature pagodas.

Above the buildings is a ramshackle garden, where gaps beneath huge boulders host a grotto, and various statues. One of these statues is likely of Pei Tu, founder of the monastery and, by all accounts, a bit of a lad.

No paragon of virtue, Pei Tu once stole a gold Buddha image from a house he stayed at. Though his pursuers were on horseback, he escaped on foot, and by crossing a river on his wooden bowl (Pei Tu means 'Cup Ferry'). On two occasions he was reported dead and buried, only to turn up again in another district.

Another statue is of the Laughing Buddha, who looks the sort of fellow to enjoy Pei Tu's antics. Three oranges have been set by him as an offering; the skin of one has peeled away, and it is mouldy, attracting flies and ants.

Two caretakers sweep leaves from the main paths. Other than them, I see only two monks and two visitors during my tour of the monastery.

I walk down the road to Tuen Mun, then take a taxi across town, to the end of the Maclehose Trail, just south of the Hoh Fuk Tong Centre. From here, a footpath leads up beside a rubbish-strewn stream, passing shanty housing behind wire fencing.

'Stranger in town!' barks a dog. Soon, all the fenced-in dogs are chorusing their disgust at the foreigner; five of them follow angrily as I walk past, thrusting their noses at the fence and snarling. Don't they realise I write for the finest animal welfare magazine in town?

The path leaves the shanties and dogs, and reaches a junction. I have a choice: the Tuen Mun Trail is to the left, the final stage of the Maclehose Trail to the right.

No contest, I reckon: after all, who wants to spend a leisure day in and around Tuen Mun? Not me.

While the Maclehose Trail crosses some tough terrain in the east, here it runs alongside a water catchment. Some tired, sore, aching trailwalkers must have passed along here. Maybe also some tired, sore, aching exercise freaks. This stretch of the catchwater has been designated an exercise trail, with numbered stops for doing pushups, pullups, plankwalking, hopping and jumping. I believe you are supposed to jog between stops.

I pass a man doing Tai Chi, a slow motion ballet that looks healthy for mind and body.

The trail is slow to escape Tuen Mun. The buildings are tightly packed; between them, I notice no greenery, only roads. Then, there are clusters of high-rises, interspersed with some semblance of countryside, as well as a highway, and stacks of containers making money for 'farmers'.

Across the sea channel is north Lantau, where work is underway on the new airport project. Before long, it will likely mirror the soulless urban blight below me.

Above the catchment, the hillside is dotted with boulders, and plants struggle to survive in soil eroded after fires. Streams run in to the channel; I rinse my face in the cool water.

Eventually, there is scrub, and occasional woodland, on both sides of the trail. I reach the Tai Lam Chung Reservoir. Here, the Maclehose Trail heads along the north shore, before an uphill climb to Route Twisk. I turn south, along a path that roughly follows the shore of the reservoir.

There is forest here, but it is thin, and seems to have an uncertain grip on the land. The earth shores of the reservoir are yellow; the ground underfoot is also pale and stony. I am reminded of places classed as semi-desert. But they are naturally formed: here, the culprit is man with his fires.

In the shade of a picnic site, I find a group of old folk making music: one plonks out a rough tune on a keyboard, while another drones into a microphone.

I turn down a road leading away from the reservoir. This passes through a correctional services centre. There is a fountain with clear blue pools; hot from my walk, I want to frolic in it. Then, a swimming pool with cool blue lining. I want to swim in it.

But I don't want to be corrected. So I avert my gaze, and walk on by.

Getting there

To reach Castle Peak Monastery, walk or take a taxi from Tuen Mun. From the Tai Lam Chung Reservoir, there are paths leading to Castle Peak Road, where buses or taxis can be caught to Tuen Mun or Tsuen Wan.

The Countryside Series map *North-West New Territories* is useful.

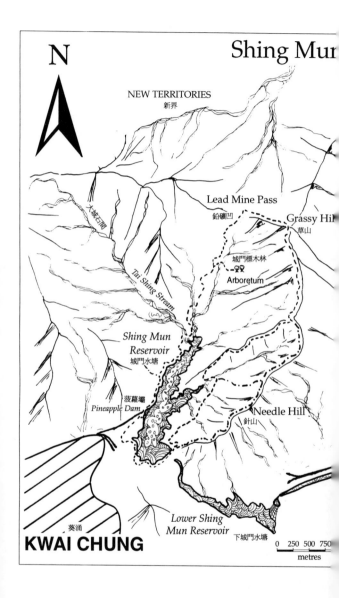

N

NEW TERRITORIES
新界

大埔凹間

Lead Mine Pass
鉛礦凹

Grassy Hill
草山

Tai Shing Stream

城門標木林
Arboretum

Shing Mun
Reservoir
城門水塘

波蘿壩
Pineapple Dam

Needle Hill
針山

葵涌
KWAI CHUNG

Lower Shing
Mun Reservoir

下城門水塘

0 250 500 750

metres

Shing Mun

Full circle   *10.5km*

After climbing the steps beside Pineapple Dam, I look out over the Shing Mun Reservoir. Surprisingly, it seems nearly empty; has there been some weird, localised drought in this area?

I walk along the Pineapple Dam Nature Trail, which makes for an easy — and pleasant — start to my outing. It starts at the dam (named after the pineapple groves of drowned villages), passes a picnic site where a woman is feeding a troop of macaques, and winds north alongside Shing Mun Reservoir.

The trail ends at a service road, and I turn right. Forest hides the reservoir. I pass through stands of tall paper-bark trees; though less than half a century old, they appear venerable, with grey, peeling bark.

A picnic site among the trees is sited on the former paddyfields of Cheung Uk Tsuen, one of the eight villages whose inhabitants were moved out when the reservoir was built. Below it, the Tai Shing Stream empties into the reservoir.

The road crosses the stream, bears sharp left, and straightens above another broad stream. At a junction, I turn left, towards Lead Mine Pass.

The road climbs, though only gently. It is being improved and, where work has halted, damp patches attract mineral-hungry butterflies. Most are large, dark swallowtails, which fly up as I approach, flashing iridescent blue wing patches.

A branch above the road sways, as a macaque walks along it, then jumps to a tree on the opposite side of the road. I hear a chestnut bulbul, a bird which only recently colonised Hong Kong. Or, like the rhesus macaque, recolonised — these bulbuls may have been common here before the original forests were destroyed.

The maturing forest is allowing some semblance of the area's former wildlife to reclaim the land. For mammals and reptiles, this mostly means an increase in the species which weathered man's onslaught. Species such as pangolins, palm civets, barking deer and pythons. Elephants, tigers and other grand beasts are surely gone for good — the South China tiger is close to extinction. The rhesus macaque, which perhaps also disappeared from the New Territories, was luckier: today's troops may all be descendants of escapees and released animals.

Birds too may escape, find Hong Kong to their liking, and breed. Some forest specialists, like the chestnut bulbul, might visit and take up residence. While their arrivals are well documented at the Tai Po Kau forest reserve, few birdwatchers bother with Shing Mun. Yet, as indicated by the chestnut bulbul, and a Hainan blue flycatcher and pair of yuhinas I see feeding young, visits can be well rewarded.

Besides aliens such as paper-bark trees, the flora includes interesting native species. Grantham's camellia, known only from Hong Kong, is found high above the reservoir. And — albeit not growing wild — in the Shing Mun Arboretum, which I reach by taking a short detour along a road to the right.

Set on four hectares of abandoned fields, the arboretum chiefly grows plants from Hong Kong and South China. Planting began in the early 1970s, and by December 1989 there were 5,070 tree and shrub specimens of 343 species. Along paths signposted to, say, FRUIT TREES, MEDICINAL PLANTS and PLANTS NAMED AFTER BOTANISTS are 37 species of bamboo, all the Hong Kong camellias, and a wide selection of local rarities.

I continue to Lead Mine Pass, with its relict name — mining lead ore from the nearby hillsides ceased a century or more ago. The pass lies roughly mid-way along the old path from Tai Po to Tsuen Wan. Today, the main path through here is the Maclehose Trail, which dips down from the east, then climbs westwards, to Tai Mo Shan.

Turning right along the Maclehose Trail, I follow a road, then a rough path up Grassy Hill. I leave the woods; this upper part of Grassy Hill is aptly named, and even those trees that do grow are little more than skeletons — victims, I guess, of fire.

Where the path meets with another restricted road, I walk to the cluster of rocks at the hill's highest point. To the north, beyond Tai Po, is Shenzhen; Kowloon lies to the south. But mostly, the view is dominated by hills — Tai Mo Shan, the Pat Sin Leng Range, Needle Hill.

I continue on the Maclehose Trail, which takes the road down from Grassy Hill along a ridge. Then the second of two roads leading off to the right. This drops to a junction near the reservoir, where I turn left, through woods sparser than those along the opposite shore.

Crossing the dam at the reservoir's southern end, I solve the mystery of the low water level in this year of rain-aplenty. Service work is evidently underway; over 70 metres below, water shoots from the dam's outlet, spraying the riverbank like a giant water cannon.

Getting there

To reach Shing Mun Reservoir, from Tsuen Wan take a red taxi or minibus 82 departing Shiu Wo Street, 150 metres south of the MTR station, or (at weekends and on public holidays) minibus 94S from Tsuen Wan Pier. The bus stop is below Pineapple Dam.

Take food and plenty to drink: there are no shops along the route.

The Countryside Series map *Central New Territories* is useful.

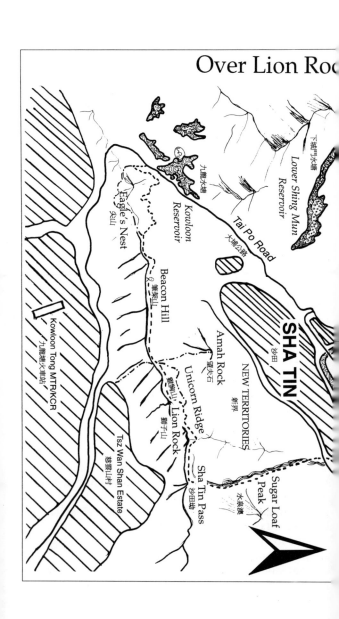

下城門水塘

Lower Shing Mun Reservoir

九龍水塘

Kowloon Reservoir

Eagle's Nest
尖山

Tai Po Road
大埔公路

Beacon Hill
畢架山

Amah Rock
望夫石

Unicorn Ridge
雞胸山

Lion Rock
獅子山

SHA TIN
沙田

NEW TERRITORIES
新界

Sha Tin Pass
沙田坳

Sugar Loaf Peak
水泉澳

Kowloon Tong MTR/KCR
九龍塘火車站

Tsz Wan Shan Estate
慈雲山村

Over Lion Rock

Soon after leaving the Tai Po Road, I see a sign by the path. WARNING — DO NOT FEED THE MONKEYS, it reads. THEY MAY ATTACK YOU AND TRANSMIT INFECTIOUS DISEASES. The message is reinforced by a photo of a fearsome looking macaque.

I turn left, along stage five of the Maclehose Trail, which here shares the same route as the Eagle's Nest Nature Trail. A tree sways above the path, as my first macaque of the morning moves to a different branch. Watching as it feeds on berries, I almost miss a much closer one, drinking from the stream beside me. Another comes down to drink; between sips, it looks nervously about, as if there might still be tigers or leopards here.

The path winds up the hillside, then levels off, to run through a fine mix of bamboo stands and young, sub-tropical forest. The sounds of traffic fade, and are lost in the all-enveloping buzzing of cicadas. I pass a second troop of macaques, then a solitary animal, sitting high in a fruiting tree. Like the others, it is well used to people, and pays little attention as I walk past.

There is a short flight of steps, leading to a ridge from where I can hear the rumbling of traffic in Kowloon. The nature trail bears right. The Maclehose Trail turns left, up Beacon Hill.

Taking the uphill path, I soon leave the woodland; shrubs grow on the exposed upper slopes. Behind me is the hill known as Eagle's Nest, where black kites, not eagles, breed. Three kites circle the hilltop.

During the reign of Emperor K'ang-Hsi (1661–1722), a lookout post was established on the summit of Beacon

Hill, with a beacon which was to be lit if attacking ships were sighted. Today, there is a radar station on the summit; the dish is enclosed in a white globe.

From Beacon Hill, the path runs down, then along the ridge towards Lion Rock, which from here appears as a sharp cone, quite unlike the resting lion profile I am used to seeing from below. I reach a junction with paths leading down and north to a catchwater or Amah Rock, and down and south to Wong Tau Han in Kowloon. Then, another junction, where the Maclehose Trail curves away round the north slopes of Lion Rock, while another path heads for the summit, 400 metres distant.

I take the Lion Rock path, which proves a tough 400 metres. At first, there are steps. But as I reach the craggy final stretch, the steps give out, and in places I scramble over the rocks. Carefully — a warning sign has no words, just an illustration of a stick man falling from an overhang.

I reach the high ridge that links three closely-spaced summits. There is a fence in front of me. Then, empty space, as the sheer south face of Lion Rock drops away. With the cliffs, crags and sharp ridge, this is surely one of the most dramatic peaks in Hong Kong.

Both Kowloon, spread beneath me to the south, and Sha Tin, to the north, seem part of a different world. Except when jet engines roar as a plane takes off from Kai Tak, only a murmur of sound carries from the city. Swifts swoop around the peak, feeding on insects carried by updraughts.

After clambering up and down the rocky western summit, I follow the ridge path eastwards. Just before a notice warning of DANGER — STEEP CLIFFS, I take a path which drops away to the north. The path is narrow, with rough steps. At the end of the path, I rejoin the Maclehose Trail, and turn right, towards Sha Tin Pass.

The Maclehose Trail affords easier walking. It does climb before reaching the pass, but up the gentle

Unicorn Ridge. Then, a downhill stretch, with estates of northern Kowloon close by on the right.

At Sha Tin Pass, there is a dai pai dong. Though I'm not hungry, I am thirsty after the walk and climb, and have nearly finished the water I brought along. I buy, and quickly down, two cans of carbonated water with flavourings and preservatives.

I have decided to leave the Maclehose Trail here, at the boundary of Lion Rock and Ma On Shan Country Parks. The easiest option would be to walk south, down to a bus terminus in Tsz Wan Shan estate. But, from my map, a path running north looks more interesting. It is one of the old footpaths which linked the Kowloon area with what is now the New Territories, and follows a stream towards Sha Tin.

At first, the stream is small. But, with water trickling and flowing in from either side, it soon grows. After a barbecue site, a path leads to a pool below a waterfall; I find it an excellent place to bathe in the cool water, and rest before continuing to Sha Tin.

Getting there

To reach the trail leading from Tai Po Road, take bus 72 from Jordan Road Ferry, or a taxi from Kowloon Tong MTR/KCR station, and get out above Kowloon Reservoir, just after a footbridge.

From the bottom of the valley from Sha Tin Pass, walk or take a taxi to Sha Tin KCR station.

Take plenty to drink: the only place selling drinks (and food) en route is at Sha Tin Pass.

Be careful on Lion Rock (you could omit the paths to and from the summit by keeping to the Maclehose Trail).

The Countryside Series map *Central New Territories* is useful.

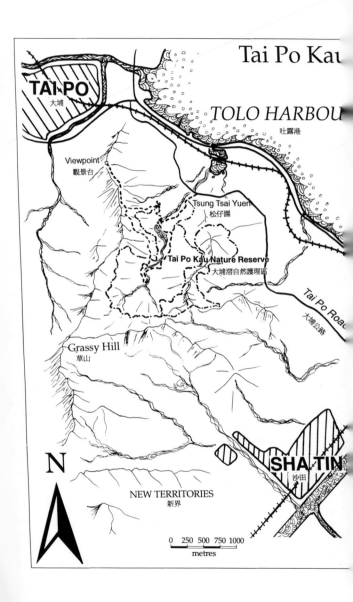

Tai Po Kau

There's forest in them thar hills   *6.5km*

Tai Po Kau Nature Reserve is one of my favourite places in Hong Kong. Yes, this is partly as it is a prime site for my hobby-cum-obsession, birdwatching. But also, I enjoy the forest, and the escape from the pell-mell of city life.

The entrance to the reserve is at a layby beside the old Tai Po Road. From here, an access road leads into a forested valley.

A couple of hundred metres up the road is the start of a nature trail. Coupled with a trail booklet, this affords a chance to learn of the workings of a tropical forest — of saplings competing for spaces in the canopy where older trees have fallen, of trees with buttress roots to support them when they are old and huge, and of the sparse undergrowth of a real 'jungle'.

But I know all that. Or anyway, I'm not interested in being educated today. Today, I will walk one of the four longer trails through the reserve.

These trails start near a dam, where water from the stream tumbling through the reserve is spirited away to catchment tunnels, and reservoirs. Without the forest, there might be no water on many days; mad muddy torrents on others. And without water — or Hong Kong's need for it — there would be no forest.

By the middle of last century, Hong Kong was largely deforested. As the population — and the territory's thirst — grew, reservoirs were built; above them, swathes of trees were planted, to absorb the brunt of rain storms, and leak out precious water during dry spells. Many were felled during the Japanese occupation, but afterwards tree planting restarted apace. And someone had the farsighted idea of making Tai Po Kau a special area, with a splendid mix of mostly native trees.

Thanks to this mix, the reserve is rich in wildlife. There are civets, wild pigs, pangolins, a host of reptiles and amphibians. The Atlas moth — world's largest moth by wingspan — lives here. So do birdwing butterflies.

There are plenty of birds, too. Mostly, I hear but don't see them — the ringing 'koo loo' of barbets, effervescent bulbuls, songs and squawks of laughing thrushes. Press a button on a listening post near the dam, and it will play a tape with selected bird sounds. Seconds after it is finished, I guess you will have forgotten which bird made which call. Better, then, to just enjoy the sounds of the forest. And walk a trail.

After running beside the stream, the path turns left and a little uphill. Then, a choice.

There are four marked trails — brown, yellow, blue and red. All loop back to the dam. A map and signpost show the brown and yellow trails heading uphill; they wind around the higher slopes of the reserve.

I prefer the blue and red trails: they are shorter and easier, and pass through the finest forest. Sometimes, I combine them, walking part way along the blue, then crossing to the red.

Today, it's the blue trail for me. Not that I have to decide now anyway, they run together for some time.

A few minutes' walk brings me to the picnic site, where wooden tables with benches have been set out in a grassy clearing. Maybe because barbecues are banned (lest they ignite the forest), I rarely find more than a handful of people here; often there is no one.

I walk on. The forest becomes dense, with tangled creepers, palms and saplings. Here, it is easy to imagine fearsome snakes like cobras, kraits, and constricting pythons suddenly attacking, as they do in B-grade jungle movies. But they are shy, and I am yet to see any in the reserve.

Leaves rustle as skinks dash for cover. Occasionally on summer visits, I glimpse non-venomous snakes. Once, a changeable (or crested tree) lizard waited by the path while I photographed it, then stalked off to find insects in some hidden place.

Another map and signpost mark the place where the red trail crosses the stream, and disappears to my right. My blue trail continues, also crosses the stream, almost doubles back on itself, then takes me uphill.

The wide, well-kept path levels off. Gaps in the trees afford views across the valley, which is like a green basin on these moist, easternmost slopes of Tai Mo Shan.

Then, there are three trails together, as brown and yellow merge from the left. I am soon back on the access road; the dam is close by.

A signpost indicates a path to a view point. Just metres from the road, this leaves the trees. To the north, the slopes are grassy, savaged by fires: a desolate reminder of the devastation wrought on Hong Kong's former forests, and of how special this reserve is.

More steps, and the path reaches the top of a hill. I had guessed the promised viewpoint would be here; but no, it is further on, and below me.

Not that I find the viewpoint a better vantage. And, with the glass smashed and map missing, I have to identify the landmarks myself. Tai Po and Tolo Harbour are easy enough; so too the Pat Sin Leng range beyond Tai Po, and Tai Mo Shan to my rear.

I return to the road. With the red walk emerging from the trees, the trails are reunited. I continue on past the dam, and down the gentle slope to the layby.

Getting there

The reserve is conveniently reached by taxi from Tai Po Market KCR station; ensure this takes you to the reserve (stop at Tsung Tsai Yuen), not Tai Po Kau village. Alternatively, walk under the bridge left of the taxi rank, north 200 metres to Tai Po Road, cross over and catch any of buses 70, 72, 72A, 73A or 74A, and alight at Tsung Tsai Yuen.

To return to the KCR station, hail a taxi at the main road (you rarely need to wait more than a few minutes for one), or take a minibus or bus to the nearest stop in Tai Po. There are also Kowloon-bound minibuses and buses.

A stall at the layby sells drinks, biscuits, and noodles with spam and egg; there are no shops or stalls in the reserve. For something fancier, the Yucca De Lac (telephone 2692-1835) restaurant, south of the Chinese University on Tai Po Road has tables on a terrace overlooking Sha Tin and Tolo Harbour. Cantonese dishes predominate.

The trails are clear and well marked, but if you want a map, take the Countryside Series map *Central New Territories*. There is a booklet on the nature trail.

Sections of the brown and yellow trails, especially, can be slippery when wet.

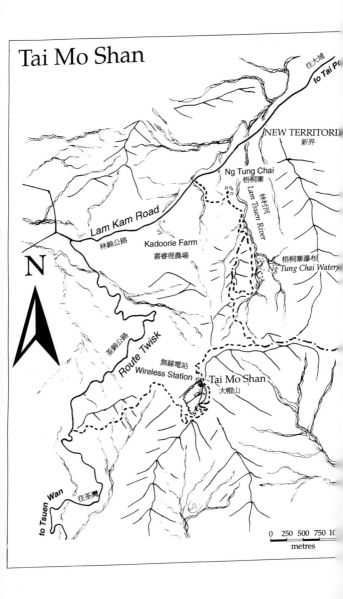

Tai Mo Shan

Walking in waterfall city   8.5km

The taxi turns off Route Twisk, and stops. 'Over-heating,' says the driver. 'The engine hasn't enough power.' Thwarted in my plans to reach the Tai Mo Shan road barrier by car, I curse, pay, and start walking.

Though a nuisance, as it is all uphill, the bonus walk is scenic, with the upper cone of Tai Mo Shan looming over high valleys, and Hong Kong Island away to the south. The view is not idyllic; on this still morning, a haze of yellow pollution hangs over the city.

But I am above the haze, in cooler, fresher air. I reach the barrier, walk around it, and start on the winding restricted road to the top. Only occasionally do I pass trees, which cling to narrow gullies offering protection from wind and fire. Grass dominates the slopes. There are boulders, too — maybe some are the former travelling stones, which started towards Tsuen Wan, there to improve the fung shui, but came to a halt when they were seen by a pregnant woman. Or so the story goes.

I reach the highest accessible point, by the entrance to the wireless station on the summit. Before this was built, seasoned hikers reportedly enjoyed the sight of newcomers reaching the top of Tai Mo Shan, and tumbling into a concealed hole.

Then, down, past an installation where a sign warns that, if I do not stop when challenged, I may be shot. I turn right, along a narrow road.

The landscape here seems wild, with rolling, green hills ahead, and valleys plunging away to left and right. But man helped shape it, felling trees and building the terraces which pattern the slopes.

At a junction with a map board and signpost, I head off to the left, towards Ng Tung Chai and the Lam Kam Road. I follow a footpath with stone steps, and cross two streams which, though innocuous today, could be dangerous when in flood.

I reach a north-facing spur, with benches for picnickers. Nearby on the left is Kadoorie Farm's eccentric signpost to the world's poles, cities, and Wanchai.

There are two paths to the Lam Kam Road. The one which promises to be most interesting, via Ng Tung Chai Waterfall, is slightly longer. Starting along it, I pass a sign which warns DIFFICULT TERRAIN: CAUTION. (In early 1995, a landslide blocked a section of this path; though now marked ROAD CLOSED, I found it could be traversed with care.)

The trail is easy at first, curving into a valley which was on my right. Abruptly, as I enter trees, it becomes a woodland path. And no longer level.

Steps lead down the steep slope, to the foot of the first in a series of waterfalls. The water spreads into a broad, white fan as it descends the Scattered Fall. By the plunge pool is the dark entrance of an abandoned mine. Just below it, I cross the stream, not needing the help of a rope and a chain slung from metal posts.

The stream disappears into space. The path leaves it, and angles steeply down through a damp world of mossy trees and crags. A small stream plunges over a low cliff to my right. (The landslide occurred here; a steep, rough track leads over the rocks and stones, rejoining the original trail after about 20 metres.) I turn back towards the first stream, and another waterfall — the Main Fall — comes into view.

A broad column of white drops perhaps 20 metres, ricochets into spray, and enters a pool where I splash in the cool water. Again, I cross the stream, and turn down. Again, I find a waterfall, this time the Middle Fall.

The stream leaving it is quiet, then surges once more as it drops into a chasm, and is lost in darkness.

I take a right turn, and find myself near the stream's exit from the chasm. It cascades out, forms a large, deep pool, and continues, more subdued, through the ravine.

Back to the main path, which no longer clings to the stream. I pass a temple that appears brand new, and walk a concrete path. On my right are fields and farmhouses. And the stream, now wide and quiet, the main tributary of the Lam Tsuen River.

At the village of Ng Tung Chai, I take a left turn, to follow a road down to Lam Kam Road.

Getting there

To reach the road barrier on Tai Mo Shan, take a taxi from Tsuen Wan MTR station (green taxis are cheaper than red; avoid taxis with 'not enough power'). Alternatively, bus 51 from Tsuen Wan Ferry to Kam Tin travels via Route Twisk (the road to Tai Mo Shan is on the right as the slope eases, by a sign for TAI MO SHAN COUNTRY PARK). To visit the lower and Main falls without crossing the landslide debris, take the hillside path leading down from Tai Mo Shan, then turn right and up the ravine; or walk up from Ng Tung Chai.

From Ng Tung Chai, take minibus 25K, or walk to Lam Kam Road to catch bus 64K or 65K, or a taxi, to Tai Po KCR station.

Take food and drink: there are no shops en route, though I thought the stream water safe enough to drink.

The path via the waterfalls, especially, may be slippery in wet weather, and impassable if the streams are in flood. The Tai Po Kau Management Centre, telephone 2656-1232, should be able to tell you the state of the paths.

The Countryside Series map *Central New Territories* is useful.

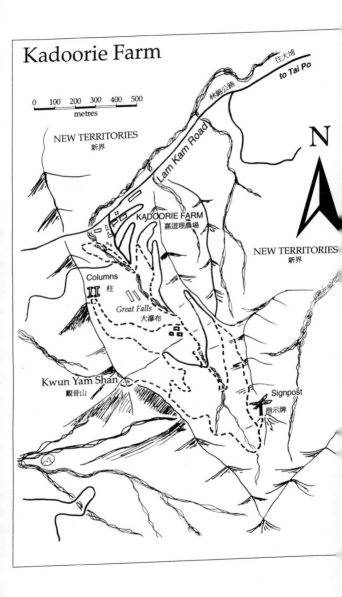

Kadoorie Farm

往大埔
to Tai Po

0 100 200 300 400 500
metres

NEW TERRITORIES
新界

林錦公路
Lam Kam Road

N

KADOORIE FARM
嘉道理農場

NEW TERRITORIES
新界

Columns 柱

Great Falls
大瀑布

Kwun Yam Shan
觀音山

Signpost
指示牌

Kadoorie Farm

Eleven miles from Wanchai   6km

Arriving at Kadoorie Farm, I check in at the reception desk and collect a map. Then, I start up the road.

I pass offices, and buildings which house an assortment of chickens (COCKS SUMMER CAMP says a sign). Making the first swing of its zigzag route up the hill, the road turns left, and leads through orchards. Orchards which flourish in an area 'experts' had declared valueless.

Kadoorie Farm dates back to the 1950s, to a time when Hong Kong was recovering from war, its population swollen by refugees from newly-communist China. To help refugees and struggling Hong Kong people earn a living, the brothers Horace and Lawrence Kadoorie introduced schemes to benefit farmers.

Crucial to their efforts was Kadoorie Farm, established in 1956. It was to be a centre for breeding new varieties of crops and livestock, developing new farming techniques, and running training courses. That was the idea, anyway. First, the steep, stony hillsides procured from the government had to be planted.

Brushing aside the doubts of agriculturalists, local villagers set about transforming the area; today, the 'valueless' land, in a steep valley cut into the north of Tai Mo Shan, boasts orchards, woods and gardens. Livestock are reared low in the valley; among them are varieties which, through being better suited to local conditions, have boosted farmers' livelihoods.

Kadoorie Farm is also a centre for conservation. Especially higher in the valley, botanic gardens host a mix of foreign and native species — some were first discovered in the valley.

Where the road makes another hairpin to the left, I turn right, along a footpath signposted to the Great Falls. This path leads to the Lam Tsuen River at the heart of the valley, here fringed with a mix of garden and woodland — the gardeners have been careful to retain original trees and bamboo.

At Great Falls, the river — here just a stream — cascades down a steep rock face; where the spray lands, mosses grow on rocks and trees. There is a pavilion beside the falls, a secluded place to rest, or picnic.

I rejoin the road, which follows the stream for a while. Then, as the road bears left once more, I again take the path alongside the stream, up past another of the many waterfalls and cascades, which are in full flow after the rains. There are greenhouses here; notices warn that PLANT THIEVES WILL BE PROSECUTED.

At the road again, I turn left, and walk to a junction where I turn sharp right. Then, I take a left turn, for a short diversion to a hilltop vantage point.

From here, I can look down over the valley to the plain with Shek Kong and, in the distance, Yuen Long. There is a board with a relief map of Hong Kong. Also, perhaps the most eccentric signpost you could find on any hilltop.

Signs radiate from the tall, metal post. Each has a locality and distance on it and, at the tip, a hand with a finger pointing the way. Neither Shek Kong nor Yuen Long is mentioned. Instead, I find directions and distances for places such as the North Pole (4,665 miles away), the South Pole (7,763 miles), London (5,989 miles), Los Angeles (7,230 miles) and Rio de Janeiro (10,992 miles). Wanchai, to the south, is 11 miles away.

Back at the road, I continue uphill, then swing round the head of the valley, and gently down. I am above most of the trees; patches of hillside are carpeted with hydrangeas in full, blue bloom.

In front is craggy Kwun Yam Shan — Goddess of Mercy Mountain. Another diversion takes me to the 546-metre summit, some 400 metres above the farm's entrance.

HOT POTS reads a notice by the summit. This tells of vents which exhale air originating from the foot of the hill, uncooled by altitude. Measurements of the temperatures of vent air and surrounding air, says the notice, have recorded differences of around six degrees: enough, in cold weather, to lead to mysterious mists around the peak. I put my hand over a vent, and notice no change in temperature. Not that I am keen to feel warmer air today anyway.

A nearby notice tells of two stone altars: partly because of the hot pots, the hill has long been regarded as sacred. When calamity struck, or bountiful harvests were hoped for, worshippers came from the valleys below, and prayed to their gods.

Two paths circuit the crag, and give fine views. Below, Route Twisk winds its way up Tai Mo Shan, becoming lost from view when almost level with Kwun Yam Shan. The upper slopes of Tai Mo Shan are patterned with terraces. A sign suggests that they were created two centuries ago for tea growing, or maybe they are far older, and were used for growing crops in times of famine, or by settlers who found no place to live in the valleys.

Heading down, I turn left, to a sharp bend where two pairs of columns might have been props in *Ben Hur*. They are from the previous Hong Kong General Post Office, and were donated by the late Mr Y.C. Liang CBE.

Soon after the bend, I again take the path past Great Falls, and the road towards reception. After chicken coops, I walk beside the lower stretch of the stream, where there are more cascades and rock gardens blending planted vegetation with wild.

I briefly visit new aviaries, which thankfully seem modelled on the best the Urban Council has produced, check out at reception, and leave.

Getting there

Kadoorie Farm is open to the public daily except on New Year's Day, during Lunar New Year (four days), Ching Ming, the Dragon Boat Festival, the Chinese Mid-Autumn Festival (the day after), Chung Yeung, and on Christmas Day. There is no entry fee. Visits should be booked in advance — telephone 2488-1317; confirmation letters are required for groups of over 10.

Bus routes 64K and 65K terminate at Tai Po KCR station, with stops on the Lam Kam Road, beside the Kadoorie Farm main entrance, or take a taxi from Tai Po KCR station (to 'Ka Doo Lay Nung Cheung' in Cantonese). Except on Sundays, if you travel by car and you have booked, you can drive on the farm roads.

Maps are available at reception; nearby is a canteen serving non-vegetarian meals, and outside that machines dispensing soft drinks.

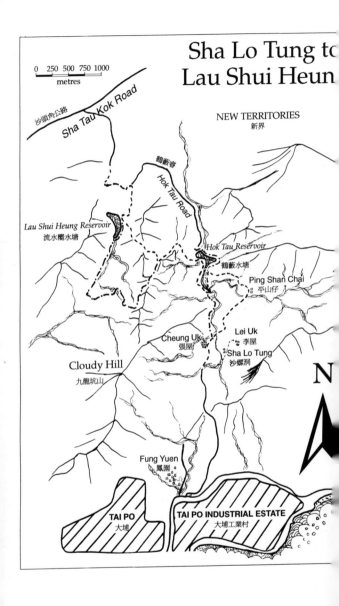

Sha Lo Tung to
Lau Shui Heun

0 250 500 750 1000
metres

沙頭角公路 Sha Tau Kok Road

NEW TERRITORIES
新界

鶴藪凹 Hok Tau Road

Lau Shui Heung Reservoir
流水嚮水塘

Hok Tau Reservoir
鶴藪水塘

Ping Shan Chai
平山仔

Lei Uk
李屋

Cheung Uk
張屋

Sha Lo Tung
沙螺洞

Cloudy Hill
九龍坑山

N

Fung Yuen
鳳園

TAI PO
大埔

TAI PO INDUSTRIAL ESTATE
大埔工業村

Sha Lo Tung to Lau Shui Heung

Now you see it, soon you won't   5.5km

Though only short, the road to Sha Lo Tung links two very contrasting places — the wealth- and pollution-generating Tai Po Industrial Estate, and a rural back-water which, one day soon, may be transformed to also generate wealth, and pollution.

As my taxi turns onto the road, I pass a yard piled with rusting metal. A sign warns that the road is narrow and winding — drivers should take care — and I start on the long uphill stretch. A plantation hides the view, and I emerge to find industry and scrapyards are well behind. Then, a right turn through a gully, and to the road's end at a tiny car park, where there is little more than an emergency phone, and an information board which no longer has information.

A concrete footpath runs behind the board, and northwards across still tranquil Sha Lo Tung. Beside it is an old rice field, recolonised by flowers and shrubs.

Groves of imposing bamboo fringe the path. Then, I reach the open expanse of the Sha Lo Tung basin. Perhaps always marshy, the basin was home to genera-tions of rice farmers. But in the 1970s, city life proved more attractive than rural, and the paddies fell into disuse. Cocooned in Pat Sin Leng Country Park, Sha Lo Tung looked set to return to a wild state.

Until, that is, golf course and housing plans were made public, and Sha Lo Tung became a battleground between conservationists and developers, in a case highlighting the risks of keeping villagers' houses and farmland outside country park boundaries. Though the territory's green groups were heartened when plans for the golf course were withdrawn in 1994, in summer 1995, former residents bulldozed abandoned fields, claiming they would restart farming if development did not begin soon. Though vegetation was cleared, trees tumbled and mud churned, neither agriculture nor building has yet ensued.

At least the development plans included preservation of villages. The terrace of Lei Uk, seemingly abandoned only months ago, looks ready-made for the museum proposed there.

Cheung Uk, which I walk past, is still home to some old folk from the Cheung clan. It nestles beneath a guardian fung shui wood, where fine trees serve as reminders of forest long gone — and the area's potential for a very different 'development', as a sanctuary for nature, an outdoor recreation centre for anyone willing to pay the price of a bus or taxi ride.

The path bears right at Cheung Uk, then offers a short cut to Hok Tau Reservoir. Rather than take this, I walk on between the paddies, cross a low ridge, and enter a valley which also has abandoned fields. The valley dwellers must have moved out long ago: there is a fung shui wood, though no village, at Ping Shan Chai. Cutting into the steep southern slopes of the Pat Sin Leng range, the valley seems wild and remote, yet is only minutes away from the road at Hok Tau.

I cross a stream by stepping stones, walk through the wood, then take the path to Hok Tau. Just before the reservoir, there are barbecue sites, and a junction with the Hok Tau Family Trail, which loops round the reservoir.

I turn left, along the family trail. Soon, this turns sharp right, and down, to cross two streams flowing into the reservoir. Then up again, and right.

The second stream, from Sha Lo Tung, has carved a twisting gorge on its way from the basin; I hear the water tumbling over cascades I can only glimpse through trees.

Approaching the reservoir again, I find a trail towards Lau Shui Heung Reservoir, two kilometres (or

¾ hour) away, according to a signpost; I am just 15 minutes from Hok Tau Road.

This new trail, part of the Wilson Trail, first climbs the hillside, taking me away from the woodland of the valley. Opposite, Pat Sin Leng's craggy peaks loom over Hok Tau.

The trail levels off, and curves below hilltops covered in shrubs and grasses. To the north, across a plain and low hills, are the high-rises of downtown Shenzhen.

Another junction with another family trail — this time a circuit of Lau Shui Heung. To the left, this trail runs towards Cloudy Hill, then reaches Bird's Pass before returning to the reservoir. But I take the shorter option, to the right.

Like Hok Tau, Lau Shui Heung Reservoir is small, set among steep hills with wooded lower slopes. Peaceful, too: the only building I notice here is a country park information hut.

A rest at the hut, then I walk down the road and right, away from the reservoir. Reaching a junction, I turn left, towards Sha Tau Kok Road, passing market gardens with flowers and ornamental trees. A taxi halts, and takes me to Fanling KCR station.

Getting there

From Tai Po KCR station, take a taxi to Sha Lo Tung; or bus 75K to the old Fung Yuen Primary School just before Tai Po Industrial Estate, and walk up the road beside the scrapyard, which turns sharp right, then left and uphill. From Lau Shui Heung Reservoir, walk to the first road junction: here you can catch minibus 52K, or maybe a taxi, to Fanling KCR station.

The trails described are well kept, and signposted.

The Countryside Series map *North-East New Territories* is useful.

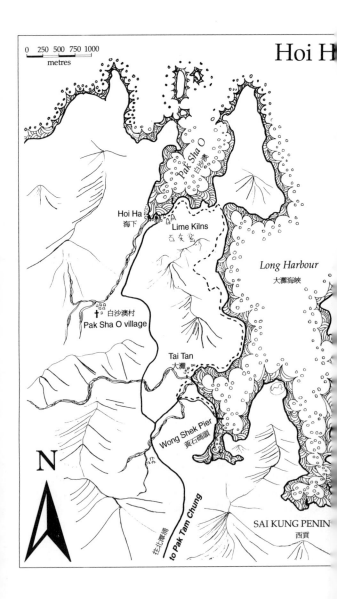

0   250 500 750 1000
metres

Pak Sha O 白沙澳

Hoi Ha
海下

Lime Kilns
石灰窰

Long Harbour
大灘海峽

† 白沙澳村
Pak Sha O village

Tai Tan
大灘

Wong Shek Pier
黃石碼頭

N

往北潭涌
to Pak Tam Chung

SAI KUNG PENIN
西貢

Hoi Ha

Hi ho, Hoi Ha   *6km*

Though not stunning, the landscape the minibus from
Pak Tam Chung passes through is pleasant and rural.
There are hills, fields, woods with dead and dying pine
trees among a rising tide of deciduous growth. Few
buildings are in view — most memorable is the church
I glimpse in the valley at Pak Sha O: an unlikely sight
out here, I think.

The minibus runs down to Hoi Ha, and stops at a
small car park. I walk through the village, along a track
leading between Spanish-style villas and a couple of
none-too-fancy restaurants. Soon, I am at the beach.

Hoi Ha faces out across an inlet (also named Pak Sha
O), towards the mouth of Tolo Harbour. The beach is
scenic — a broad arc backed by hills — but hardly
idyllic, with drab sand and a dusting of dark silt just
below the tideline.

Nevertheless, people are paddling, swimming and
picnicking. There are also weekend campers; some
have already packed up and gone, leaving piles of
plastic bags and tins. Just metres away, a litter bin is
half empty.

I walk back into the village, and turn left, passing
older houses and a small temple or ancestors' hall.
Then, through a fung shui wood.

There are two rebuilt lime kilns to the right of the
path. Originally built around 100 years ago, they date
from an era when coral formed the basis of a local
industry, lime making. Though gone from many parts
of Hong Kong, coral is still found at Hoi Ha, mostly
fringing the western shore, and could again form the

basis of a local industry: tourism, albeit small scale, and attracting mainly day-trippers.

Some 37 of Hong Kong's 50 coral species have been found in the inlet. 'On a calm day,' says film-maker Michael Pitts, 'you can look down from a boat and see a coral garden. There are brain corals, pinnacle and plate corals, anemones, tube worms and peacock worms.' But few fish: not everything in the garden is lovely. The area has been overfished and, inevitably, there is pollution — sometimes making the water so murky that visibility drops to little more than a metre.

But the World Wide Fund for Nature, hoping the pollution will not worsen and the visibility will hold at the more typical three metres, has plans for Hoi Ha. The organisation is hoping to open a Marine Life Centre by the year 2000; there may also be a glass-bottomed boat to take visitors on excursions to view the marine life.

One important step in protecting Hoi Ha came when it was designated a marine park in 1996. Initially, villagers had opposed plans for the park, fearing it would mean they could no longer fish even though they barely do any fishing nowadays. But the WWF explained that they could still fish, using hooks and line, though yes, there will be areas where fishing will be prohibited. 'In New Zealand,' says Ralph Leonard of the WWF, 'fishermen were first opposed to a similar scheme, but now the area has become a treasure trove of fish.'

It seems improbable: imagine viewing coral and protected fish in Hong Kong. I hope the dreams are realised and the pollution recedes: Hong Kong would be a poorer place if the only reminders of its corals were photos, a film, and rebuilt lime kilns.

The path, which turns a little uphill beside a pier, runs through scrub, young trees and bamboo thickets. I reach the narrow neck of a peninsula. A faded sign warns people to keep off the peninsula, but the fencing is tumbledown, the gate no longer barred. Canoeists have beached below me; a yacht is moored at a quay on the peninsula, and its crew are playing volleyball.

I turn right, and south, along a hillside where fires have left little but grass and bare branches. Across Long Harbour is the easternmost part of the Sai Kung peninsula, with the distinctive profile of Sharp Peak. Tap Mun — Grass Island — comes into view as I continue southwards.

The path climbs, and runs above a craggy outcrop. Then round a corner, and down into a small valley with a small wood, and a tiny stream burbling between boulders. Up again, left at a junction, and on south, beside the inlet.

The path leads across a beach. I disturb common sandpipers which have been feeding on the rocks; they fly low over the sea, with wicking wing beats and high, 'wit wit wit' calls. They are migrants, perhaps newly arrived in Hong Kong. I count 15 — the largest flock I have seen here.

The path keeps low, and curves into a bay with mangroves lining the shore. There is a village, Tai Tan, again with Spanish-style villas, at the head of the bay.

I meet a road, and turn left, to Wong Shek Pier. There is little at the pier — barbecue sites, benches, the Jockey Club Water Sports Centre, vendors selling soft drinks, which I buy. And a bus stop, where I catch the bus to Choi Hung.

Getting there

Hoi Ha can be reached by taxi from Sai Kung or Pak Tam Chung or — on Sundays and public holidays — minibus 7 from Pak Tam Chung.

Bus 94 runs between Sai Kung and Wong Shek Pier (stopping at Pak Tam Chung); on Sundays and public holidays, there is also bus 96R between Choi Hung MTR station and Wong Shek Pier (also stopping at Pak Tam Chung).

There are small restaurants in Hoi Ha; vendors sell drinks at Wong Shek Pier (perhaps only at weekends and during holidays).

The Countryside Series map *Sai Kung and Clear Water Bay* is useful.

Chek Keng to Tai Lon

SAI KUNG PENINSULA
西貢

Chek Keng village
赤徑村

Ferry to Ma Liu Shui
往馬料水

Chek Keng Pier
赤徑碼頭

Ham Tin
鹹田

Tai Long
大浪村

Sharp Peak
蚺蛇尖

0 250 500 750 1000
metres

N

Chek Keng to Tai Long

Rucksacks on the rampage   *8km*

Though I clamber on board the ferry half an hour before the scheduled departure, it is already filling up. Rucksacks crowd aisles, gangways, spaces between seats. Rucksack bearers squeeze onto benches. More people arrive; some have to stand.

The appointed time arrives, and off we go. Tolo Harbour is calm, grey in the morning light. The expressway and towns recede; to port and starboard hills line this infamously filthy — yet still beautiful — inlet.

The ferry makes its first stop, at Sham Chung, and disgorges a goodly number of rucksacks and bearers.

Moments later, it is moving again. Another halt, then through Tolo Channel to Tap Mun (Grass Island), with its fishing boats and fish farms. Two further halts, then, around 15 minutes later than scheduled, we reach the Chek Keng pier.

I let the rucksacks leave first, walk up the steps and head along the path that leads to the village.

'Brain fever! Brain fever!! Brain fever!!!' sings a large hawk cuckoo, from a patch of woodland close by. I peer into the trees, but can't see it.

After crossing a bridge over a stream, I turn left, and up. Eventually, this path will take me to a fine beach. But first, I must cross the ridge in front.

The slope is gentle, but persistent, and with the view changing only little as I climb, I am glad to finally reach the top.

I rest on the grassy slopes, enjoying a cool breeze, and the view down to the east coast of the Sai Kung peninsula. Some rucksack bearers halt, too. But mostly they seem compelled to go on; a line of them snakes up the hill to the south, like ants labouring with full loads.

Others head down, towards the beach.

The beach: tugging me on down, too. This eastern side of the ridge is steeper, and the path zigzags. I pass burnt scrub, where the fire has revealed the stones of an old footpath.

I enter my first village of the day, Tai Long, and buy a drink from the first, basic restaurant, the First Stop. Tai Long is small, a cluster of houses with footpaths for streets. My path runs by another restaurant aimed at hikers and day-trippers, then along the level ground beside a stream.

The beach is very near. But first, I must beat the paddy. I walk into an abandoned paddyfield, and squelch around in the water and ankle-deep mud. I flush three chestnut bitterns, six or seven snipe, and a watercock. Then, having scared all the birds I can for now, back to the path.

Ham Tin lies just around a corner; it is even smaller, though less compact, than Tai Long. I turn off the path, to the right, and cross sand to a footbridge over a stream.

The bridge has a rusting, twisted skeleton of iron pipes, overlaid with a crooked jumble of wood, which looks as if gaps left by rotted planks had been hastily repaired using any old driftwood that came to hand.

The unlikely contraption holds as I cross. A filthy paddy-beater walks into the stream, to rinse feet, boots and socks.

Almost presentable again, I cross the beach to near the tideline, and watch the waves rolling in.

Offshore, there are two craggy islets. Two white-bellied eagles are perched on one of them, showing pale against the dark trees and rock. Inland, Ham Tin is mostly hidden among trees; beyond it rise Sharp Peak, and the ridge I came over.

After a late picnic lunch, I start heading back. Alongside Ham Tin I notice a restaurant overlooking the beach — the Sea View. Beside it, a short, rough track leads up and over to the superb Tai Wan beach.

Back to Tai Long, then up to the ridge, the path seeming longer going up than it did coming down. Again, I rest at the top.

Soon, I am back at the coast near the ferry pier. With time to spare, I turn left, to Chek Keng. The tide is low, and boats rest on the mud. There is another village house turned simple restaurant, where I buy another soft drink.

Like Tai Long, Ham Tin and countless other villages in Hong Kong, Chek Keng has been sapped by the drain of young people to the city. Some houses are still lived in, perhaps by old folk, others have been abandoned.

Alongside Chek Keng, cattle graze beside bushes. Rucksacks are still on the move. A girl with small rucksack and small dog comes along, and finds me staring at the hillside, still hoping to find that cuckoo. 'What are you looking at?' she asks. 'Oh, a waterfall,' she says. And she is on her way again. The waterfall is prominent, yet it seems she was not aware of it until now. Perhaps it is already forgotten, as she carries her rucksack on into the evening.

The ferry should arrive soon. I walk around to the pier, passing a group of Boy Scouts setting up camp (and getting ready for team games: they have posted signs for BUFFALO and WOODPECKER).

There is a small crowd waiting by the pier but, once the ferry has transferred people to Wong Shek, there are few on the return trip to Ma Liu Shui. The rucksacks are out for a long weekend.

Getting there

The Tolo Harbour ferry, operated by the Polly Ferry Company, (telephone 2771-1630, Cantonese only), departs the pier at Ma Liu Shui (10–15 minutes' walk from University KCR station) at 8:30 AM daily, and is scheduled to arrive at Chek Keng at 10:20 AM. The return ferry departs Chek Keng at 4:45 PM, and the journey takes a little over one hour.

You could also travel via Wong Shek Pier, catching motorised sampans between there and Chek Keng; Wong Shek Pier is served by bus 94 from Sai Kung and (on Sundays and public holidays) bus 96R from Choi Hung MTR station.

A useful map of the area is the Countryside Series map *Sai Kung and Clear Water Bay.*

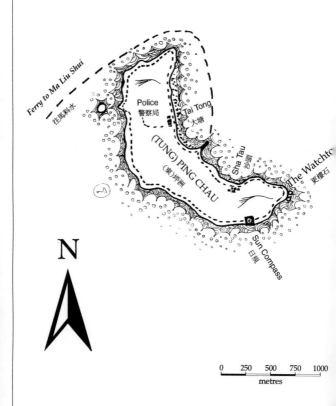

MIRS BAY

大鵬灣

Ferry to Ma Liu Shui

往馬料水

Police
警察局

Tai Tong
大塘

Sha Tau
沙頭

(TUNG) PING CHAU
(東)坪洲

The Watchto

更樓石

Sun Compass

日規

N

| 0 | 250 | 500 | 750 | 1000 |

metres

Ping Chau

The far east   *6km*

As I walk off the ferry pier, I see a notice. PASSENGERS, it says, ARE ADVISED NOT TO VISIT THE OUTLYING ISLANDS UNLESS THEY HAVE CHECKED IN ADVANCE THAT A RELIABLE MEANS OF RETURN TRANSPORT IS AVAILABLE. Sound though the advice may be, it is, I fear, too late — I am already on Ping Chau, and Hong Kong's islands do not come any more outlying than this.

By the time the ferry rounded the north coast of the island, the hills of Sai Kung and Plover Cove Country Park were little more than low shapes in the haze. Now, mainland China dominates the view. The green, hilly peninsula that bounds eastern Mirs Bay is so close that, through binoculars, I can clearly see resorts, fishing villages, roads, and people walking on beaches.

Yet while nearby Guangdong flourishes, this far-flung, improbable outpost of Hong Kong seems set on its own, contrary course. In the days when Shenzhen was barely a twinkle in the Chinese government's eyes, and the peninsula was surely little inhabited, Ping Chau's population was reportedly over 1,000. Today, with most houses abandoned and crumbling, the island is home to just two old men, and only at weekends do the remaining villages come alive.

Backpackers and daytrippers have arrived on the ferry. Also, there are island folk, who might live in new towns, but can still call Ping Chau home. Carrying provisions, they head for their houses, there to meet friends, set up stalls selling soft drinks and cooked food, and rent out beds for the night.

At Tai Tong village a little north of the pier, I book a room, and leave some belongings. Then, I set off along a footpath heading inland. It leads to a cluster of derelict houses, set in a wood where the only sounds are of bamboo swaying and scraping in the wind.

I retrace my steps, then turn left, left again before the police station — which is still in use — and find the path leads to an army training camp. This is now Hong Kong's only radiation shelter — Ping Chau is just 12 kilometres from the Daya Bay nuclear power station. Later, I find that a track skirts round the camp, and drops down to the island's west coast. But now, I turn back, and halt for lunch at the hostel.

Over lunch, I talk with a Ping Chau devotee, who has been visiting the island for over 20 years. In the early 1970s, he tells me, robberies by people from China were so frequent that everyone left; only the two old men have returned to live here. I ask about smuggling, which was, reputedly, rife. After a pause, he says only, 'That does not happen now.'

I walk to the beach, and turn left. There are stretches of fine, white sand, and outcroppings of the mudstone that makes up the island, and is found nowhere else in Hong Kong. The sea is a classic, tropical blue; coral chunks scattered along the tideline hint at the attractions of snorkelling here.

At the north end of the island, the path leaves the beach, climbs, and runs above a low cliff. Ping Chau is in the shape of a crescent, roughly two kilometres long and never more than 700 metres wide. Along its inner, eastern arc, the layers of the mudstone slope gently into the sea. But elsewhere, the rock is sliced away, forming these cliffs.

The path curves, and follows the clifftop southwards. The island's rolling landscape, no longer farmed, is carpeted with long grasses and shrubs, with woods hiding the old villages.

At the southern end of the island, I reach the highest point, a modest 48 metres above sea level. There is a 'sun compass', with arrows pointing in the directions of sunset and sunrise at different times of year.

Then, down, to a place where the cliffs have all but eroded away, leaving two stubborn, tor-like masses: the Ping Chau Watchtowers. Below them, the sea meets rock which resists in rows, or is torn away in slabs to leave erratic, zigzag steps and suddenly deep rock pools.

From here, it is only a short walk back to the hostel, and I have time to explore trails which cut across the island.

My bed for the night is basic: a solid-looking bunk, with only a bamboo mat to lie on. But after dinner and a few beers, I sleep quickly, and soundly.

I am up and out before dawn, hoping to see a good sunrise. Reaching the Watchtowers, I find others have gathered with the same intention. But there are too many clouds to the east; though some turn a promising, deep red, they soon bleach grey again, and when the sun finally appears from behind a hill, it is already an intense yellow.

I again circuit the island, reversing yesterday's route, and birdwatching — migrants are in evidence, and include a Hong Kong rarity, a Radde's warbler. A migrant hotspot, Ping Chau attracts fair densities of songbirds such as warblers, which mostly favour the small woods.

After a late breakfast at the hostel, and settling my bill, I stroll to the pier to await the ferry to Wong Shek. Looking down from the pier, I see hundreds of small fish, and rounded corals.

One ferry arrives, and berths — but it is not the one I want. Then another, and another. They must have been travelling across Mirs Bay like a small flotilla; four or five ferries berth and disgorge day-trippers. Then comes the Wong Shek ferry, which rolls in a way that seems out of all proportion to the gentle swell, and takes me back the mainland.

Getting there

The island is usually called Tung (East) Ping Chau, probably to distinguish it from Peng Chau, near Lantau, which is pronounced the same in Cantonese.

The Polly Ferry Company (telephone 2771-1630, Cantonese only) operates ferries to Ping Chau from Ma Liu Shui (10–15 minutes walk from the University KCR station); they depart at 9 AM and 3:30 PM on Saturdays and at 9 AM on Sundays; return ferries are at 5:30 PM on Saturdays and Sundays: $70 return. Especially on Sundays, the ferry may be fully booked; advance tickets are available from MTR travel service centres, including those in Admiralty, Causeway Bay, Tsim Sha Tsui and Mong Kok stations. There are also ferries during public holidays.

I left the island on a Sunday '10:30 AM' (was nearly 11 AM) ferry to Wong Shek pier, from where bus 96R leaves for Choi Hung MTR station, or there is transport via Sai Kung.

There are hostels in Sha Tau, south of the Ping Chau ferry pier, and at Tai Tong, north of the pier (if you wish to book, try calling 2661-2680, or 2661-0241, probably Cantonese only).

Food and drinks are available on the island.

There are map boards near the ferry pier and the sun compass; Ping Chau is included in the Countryside Series map *North-East New Territories*.

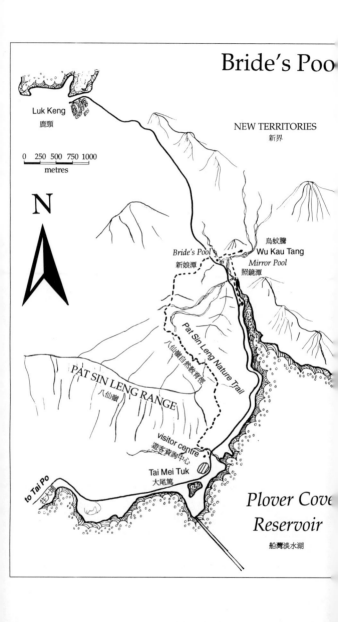

Bride's Poo

NEW TERRITORIES
新界

Luk Keng
鹿頸

0 250 500 750 1000
metres

N

Bride's Pool
新娘潭

烏蚊騰
Wu Kau Tang
Mirror Pool
照鏡潭

Pat Sin Leng Nature Trail
八仙嶺自然教育徑

PAT SIN LENG RANGE
八仙嶺

visitor centre
遊客資詢中心

Tai Mei Tuk
大尾篤

to Tai Po
往大埔

Plover Cove
Reservoir
船灣淡水湖

Bride's Pool

A tale of two nature trails 5km

Arriving at the Tai Mei Tuk visitor centre, I find it is yet to open. No matter, I doubt my day will be poorer for not seeing the exhibits. I start up the Pat Sin Leng Nature Trail, which follows a road, and crosses a water culvert.

Beside the footbridge is stop one of the trail. I have brought along the trail booklet, and find the information on stop one concerns the culvert, which is designed to limit debris entering Plover Cove Reservoir.

The first flight of steps leads up the hillside. I pause at other numbered markers, and read the corresponding entries in the booklet. Though the markers look new, the information is dated. Rotting tree stumps, ferns and hillside views are now obscured by a vigorous growth of shrubs. Quartz, says the booklet, is a hard mineral with uses which include making needles for record players ('Daddy, what's a record player?').

I hear the cry of a bird of prey, and see a black baza cruising past at eye level. The elegant, pied bird tumbles down through the air, and swoops low over the valley. A second baza joins in the display. Bazas are among the birds which have colonised Hong Kong as woodland has improved; maybe this pair will nest in the secluded valleys of this northeastern corner of Hong Kong.

Plover Cove Reservoir dominates the view. Built in the 1960s, it helped put an end to not infrequent, drastic water rationing. Though the reservoir is still far from capacity, the water level is higher than when I last saw it; rocky islets are almost submerged.

The path winds in and out of gullies with stands of bamboo. A signpost points to Pat Sin Leng, half an hour away. But, reckoning I have climbed enough for today, I am not tempted; the nearest peak of the Pat Sin Leng range is 170 metres higher than this junction.

A craggy bluff hides the reservoir. Eastwards is Wu Kau Tang; the Mirror Pool waterfall pours into the ravine below it. Though over 1½ kilometres distant, I can hear the surging water.

Above and beyond Wu Kau Tang, Mirs Bay is just visible, but mists shroud Ping Chau. To the north lies Sha Tau Kok, split by the border, and looking more modern and developed on its Chinese side.

The slopes the trail passes are uninhabited, and mostly covered in dense scrub, or young woods. Opposite, there are only patches of woodland, but great expanses of charred hillside, or grass where there has been respite from fire for a few months. Though hikers and picnickers pass through here, it seems they have little impact on the environment compared to villagers who show scant regard for the land in which they live.

The trail starts heading down. I cross a stream flowing through a narrow, wooded ravine, climb a little, and turn off to the right, to sit on a hilltop, eat, and rest before the final downhill section.

There are steps down to the road linking Tai Mei Tuk with Luk Keng, and the end of the trail. The trail booklet has a 'note for hearty walkers' pointing out that the Pat Sin Leng and Bride's Pool Nature Trails can be combined. Hearty walker that I am, I plan to do just this; I can see the start of the Bride's Pool trail across the road.

But first, time for an ice cream, sold by one of the stalls set up to cater for weekend visitors.

And so to the Bride's Pool trail. This crosses the stream, then takes me along the valley side above the waterfall plunging into the pool. Maybe this is the path from which the legendary bride-to-be fell to her doom, when one of the bearers carrying her sedan chair slipped and tipped her down the steep slopes to the stream below.

I reach a footbridge across a tributary flowing in from the east. Beside this is a stone tablet which says the bridge was built in 1906, with donations from Jamaica, Hong Kong, Honolulu and the United States. Chief donor was Sir Cecil Clementi, then District Officer, and later governor of Hong Kong (1925–1930).

There is a path to the left, into the ravine from which the tributary emerges. I take it, and soon arrive at the Mirror Pool waterfall. At 35 metres, this is higher than the Bride's Pool fall. More spectacular too: I once arrived after a long, rainy spell, when trees swayed in a wind pushed through the ravine by the foaming torrent. Today, the fall is quieter, and I sit on boulders near the pool, said to be used as a mirror by the spirit of the bride, who washes her hair in the stream.

The path is a dead end; I return to the nature trail. This continues down the well-wooded valley, towards Plover Cove Reservoir.

At one place, it crosses a footbridge over the outflow from a catchment tunnel. The water is quiet as it rushes from the darkness of the tunnel, but explodes into roaring whiteness as it crosses a weir beneath the bridge. Two girls seem alarmed at the sight and sound, and walk quickly on.

The trail ends at a car park. The nearest bus service is from Tai Mei Tuk, five kilometres down the road. I start on what seems an unpromising walk, and am relieved when a taxi arrives to carry me away.

Getting there

From Tai Po KCR station, bus 75K runs to Tai Mei Tuk; the start of the Pat Sin Leng Nature Trail is beside the visitor centre, next to the road about half a kilometre east of the village. From the end of the Bride's Pool trail, walk along the road back to Tai Mei Tuk in order to catch the return bus, maybe watching for passing taxis (more likely at weekends), or walk north to Luk Keng, from where minibus 56K runs to Fanling KCR station.

Take plenty of water or soft drinks: there are no permanent shops along the route.

The trails are well marked. The Countryside Series map *North-East New Territories* is useful, and has notes on the nature trails.

Bibliography

If you want to continue exploring Hong Kong's byways, you could look at some other guidebooks.

For mostly brief excursions, try *Magic Walks*, by Kaarlo Schepel. The original edition, published in 1990, was so popular it spawned volume 2a (covering Hong Kong Island) in 1990, updated in 1992, volume 3 (New Territories and Lantau) in 1992, volume 2b (Kowloon and the Outlying Islands) in 1994, and *The Maclehose Trail and Its Surroundings*, by Richard Pearce in 1995. All were published by the Alternative Press.

If you are a walking enthusiast, you should enjoy the company of Graham Heywood and Richard Gee in *Rambles in Hong Kong*. (Oxford University Press, 1992.) The text of Heywood's book, originally published in 1938, appears alongside a commentary by Gee.

The Friends of the Earth began publishing their Coastal Guide Series of walking books, including large maps and notes on wildlife, with *Lamma Island* in 1995, followed by *Lantau Island* in 1997, and *Hong Kong Island and Po Toi Island* due in late 1998.

The Maclehose Trail, text by Chris Bale, photos by Tim Nutt and paintings by Tao Ho, is a portrait of the territory's longest trail. (Chinese University Press, 1992.)

For background on rural Hong Kong, you might refer to the following:

Hong Kong Country Parks, by Stella Thrower (Government Printer, 1984), is an ageing but informative account of the country parks, which together occupy around 40 percent of Hong Kong's land area.

Leaflets on country parks are available, free of charge, from the Government Offices, Canton Road, Kowloon, as well as from the relevant country park visitor centres (which often, though, seem to be out of stock). Leaflets on Tai Po Kau, and Sai Kung, Clear

Water Bay and Shing Mun country parks are recently produced, others may be dated.

For local wildlife see *A Colour Guide to Hong Kong Animals* by Dennis Hill and Karen Phillipps, covering the commoner mammals, reptiles, amphibians and various land and freshwater invertebrates, as well as creatures inhabiting or washed up on the seashore. (Government Information Services, 1981.) *Birds of Hong Kong and South China,* by Clive Viney, Karen Phillipps and Lam Chiu Ying is the companion guide for birds. (Hong Kong Government, 1994.) Both books are available in English or Chinese versions.

The Urban Council has published several photographic guides to the local flora and fauna. Some, such as one on grasses, seem aimed at specialists; one of the more accessible guides of wider interest is *Hong Kong Amphibians and Reptiles,* by Stephen Larsen, Michael Waineng Lau and Anthony Bogadeck. (Urban Council, 1986.)

The Green Dragon, by a team of writers and photographers including Martin Williams and Michael Pitts (Green Dragon Publishing, 1994), explores Hong Kong's wildlife and wild places in words and pictures.

In Search of the Past: A Guide to the Antiquities of Hong Kong by Solomon Bard (Urban Council, 1988), describes many of Hong Kong's more interesting historical places, but not temples and archaeological sites. Sadly, it is itself somewhat dated.

The Government Publications Centre, Queensway Government Offices, Lower Block, G/F, telephone 2537-1910, has a good selection of books on Hong Kong — including titles published by Government Information Services and the Urban Council — as well as the excellent Countryside Series and other maps.

Most of the major booksellers have Hong Kong sections, though typically without the full range of government publications.

Glossary

You may find the following list of Cantonese geographical terms useful or interesting.

au	坳	pass, saddle
chau	洲	island
ha	下	lower
hang	坑	stream, valley
heung	鄉	village
ho	河	river
hui	墟	market
kok	角	headland
ling	嶺	summit
lo	老	old
miu	廟	temple
mun	門	channel
nam	南	south
o	澳	harbour, bay
pak	北	north
sai	西	west
san	新	new
sha	沙	sand
shan	山	mountain
shek	石	rock
sheung	上	upper
siu	小	small
tai	大	big
tarn	灘	beach
tau	頭	headland
tei	地	district
tsuen	村	village
tsui	咀	spit
tung	東	east
uk	屋	clan village
wai	圍	walled village
wan	灣	bay

About the author

Soon after obtaining a PhD in physical chemistry from Cambridge University, Martin Williams resolved to pursue conservation — which was closely linked to birdwatching, an obsession since his early teens, and headed to Beidaihe on the northeast coast of China as leader of a team studying autumn bird migration.

After travels in search of birds in Beidaihe and southern China, Williams settled in Hong Kong to work as a freelance writer and photographer. He has since appeared in publications including *BBC Wildlife, Discovery,* the *Far Eastern Economic Review, Geo, New Scientist, Newsweek, Mandarin Oriental, Pacific Discovery, Reader's Digest* and *Wildlife Conservation.* He was the chief writer for, and a contributing photographer to, the books *The Green Dragon: Hong Kong's living environment,* and the Friends of the Earth Coastal Guide *Hong Kong Island and Po Toi Island.*

Williams has also continued to visit Beidaihe at most years, leading further surveys and birdwatching tours. In 1996 he was part of a team surveying biodiversity in the vicinity of Ertan, a huge dam being built in southwest Sichuan province.

He now plans a book on his experiences at Beidaihe. Other ideas include working on television documentaries, and further travels from his Cheung Chau base to cover the Far East's wildlife and wild places in words and pictures.

Other titles from Asia 2000

Non-fiction

Fiction

Poetry

Order from Asia 2000 Ltd
302 Seabird House, 22–28 Wyndham St,
Central, Hong Kong
tel (852) 2530 1409; fax (852) 2526 1107
email: sales@asia2000.com.hk; http://www.asia2000.com.hk/

HONG KONG PATHFINDER